Welcome!

I am so glad you are here! This whole journey of choosing *Faith Over Fear* has been a big one for me. I have battled fears and anxieties for as long as I can remember. Even as a young girl (who shouldn't have many fears or anxieties), I claimed Philippians 4:6-7 as my life verses. In summary they say, "Don't worry about anything, pray about everything." I have clung to these verses so often throughout my life, but in the past year, fear really started to grip me in new ways. And I know I'm not alone.

In this study, I want to share with you some of my experiences and some of the tangible things I did to fight fear. I want to give you specific strategies that will help grow your faith. I truly believe that fear is part of the spiritual warfare that is constantly going on. Fear starts in the mind and the Bible clearly tells us to "renew our minds." We have got to work at it. It doesn't happen automatically. But I can tell you from experience... God CAN and WILL take away the fear that seems to consume you. If only you will BELIEVE that He can do it, and then DO the work to replace the fears in your head with the Truth of Scripture.

This is going to be fun, y'all! Not only are we renewing our minds, we are also gonna grow our art skills... because after all, we were created to create! And it's just fun! Plus, when you can beautifully display the scripture cards at your work, in your car, on your bathroom mirror, on your fridge, or wherever... when you put those words in front of you on a daily basis, it helps get them into your mind, and that is what helps renew the mind.

So let's do this, y'all!! Let's draw, let's paint, let's write, let's dive into scripture, and most importantly - let's choose to believe that God is who He says He is and there 'ain't nothing too hard' for Him!!

Kasey Hope

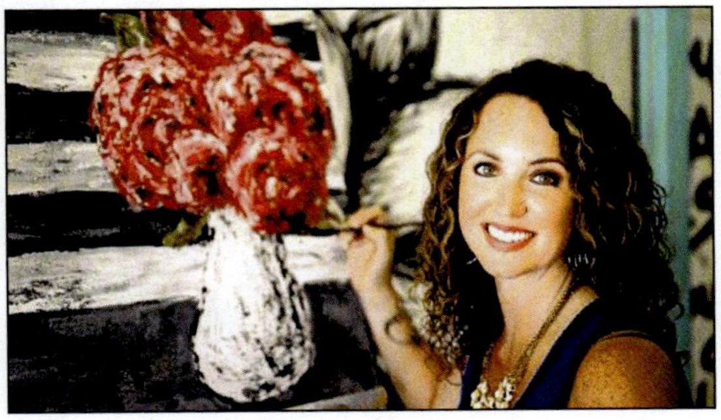

Kasey Hope is an licensed artist, teacher, and entrepreneur. She opened P'zazz Art Studio in central Alabama in the summer of 2007. Since then she has taught art to thousands of children and adults.

Her studio is partnered with Rice Bowls (www.ricebowls.org) to help provide food for orphans around the world. To date, P'zazz has been able to provide over 70,000 meals to kids in need. Your purchase of this book helps that number to keep growing!!

WEEK ONE: PARALYZED

I will never forget the May afternoon that I took my small children to the pool for my daughter's end-of-the-year party for her preschool class.

Everybody was having so much fun. Parents were chatting, kids were jumping on jumpies, and then we moved to the pool to begin swim time. That's when it occurred to me: although my daughter could swim… I also had my 2-year-old son with me. He was fine just being my side-kick but when I saw the other kids swimming, I felt bad that I hadn't brought him any swim-mies or a life jacket or anything.

That's when a sweet mom friend told me we could bor-row hers. I strapped the the swimmy on my son. It was the kind that had stacked pads on the back and strapped around his chest. I thought it seemed kinda awkward, but I knew they used these type of things to teach kids to swim… so surely it would be fine. We put him on the slide and he slid down right into the water. To my horror, he landed face-first in the water and because of the extra padding on his back he couldn't quite pull himself up out of the water.

I just stood in shock and disbelief and then my feet didn't seem to know how to move, but evidently my right arm did… with my right arm, I pushed the lifeguard in the water and just yelled "GET HIM!"

I felt like the lifeguard took for-ever to jump in and get my son. Thankfully, after some coughing and calming down, he was fine. But man, in that moment, I was so so scared.

[Fear overtook my body and it felt as if it just paralyzed me. I couldn't move.]

I didn't jump in to save my son. MY job is to protect my son… yet FEAR stopped me! I was so mad at myself after it was all over.

Isn't that what fear always does though? It paralyzes us. It stops us from doing the very things we were made to do. It stops us from being fully obe-dient to God. It stops us from believing God and stepping into what He's called us to do. Fear is NO good!!!

What does 2 Timothy 1:7 say about fear? ____________________

____

____

Fear is not from whom?

____

What does the Spirit of God give us according to verse 7?

____

____

I don't know about you, but I will take power, love and self-dis-cipline over fear any day!! And y'all… that's what's in store for you!!! When you allow the Holy Spirit to come and do the work that only He can do, that fear is replaced with power, with love, with self-discipline and with peace!! That's some good news!!!!

So before we get too far into this, I want you to take a minute. **Be honest.** What fears are currently in your life that are holding you back and paralyzing you from moving into what God wants for you? We have to name it before we can fight it! So go ahead. **Take some time.** Ask God to reveal to you areas where you are letting fear win.

Now, I want you to dig into scripture. Psalms 34:4 says, "I sought the Lord. He answered me. He delivered me from all my fears." That's what we are going to do! **We are going to seek God.** So in the space below, seek His Word, the Bible. Find verses that speak specifically to the fears you are dealing with. If you aren't sure where to begin, simply Google "verses that deal with fear" or "verses that deal with fear of ________."

Begin keeping a list of the verses that speak specifically to you. God is a personal God. He has a personal Word for YOU. So open that Bible and dig it. Record your verses here!!

1 ________

2 ________

3 ________

4 ________

5 ________

6 ________

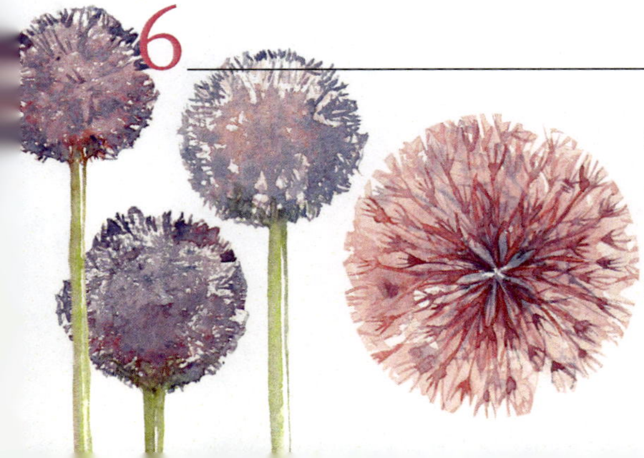

If you are doing this study in a group, you may want to share your list with your group; your fears and your fighting verses. This isn't a time for you to be embarrassed. This is spiritual warfare that we are dealing with here. And as sisters in Christ, we need to be praying for each other. So take some time to share these fears and pray over one another.

HANDWRITING Technique

Adding a Swoosh

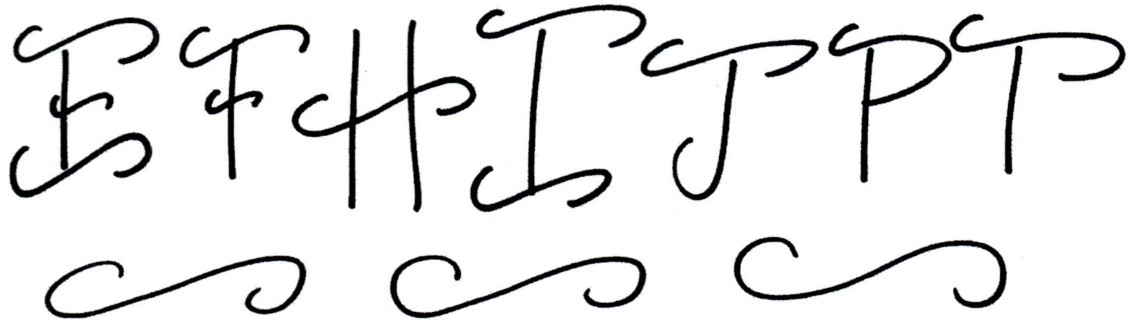

Thickening the Downstrokes

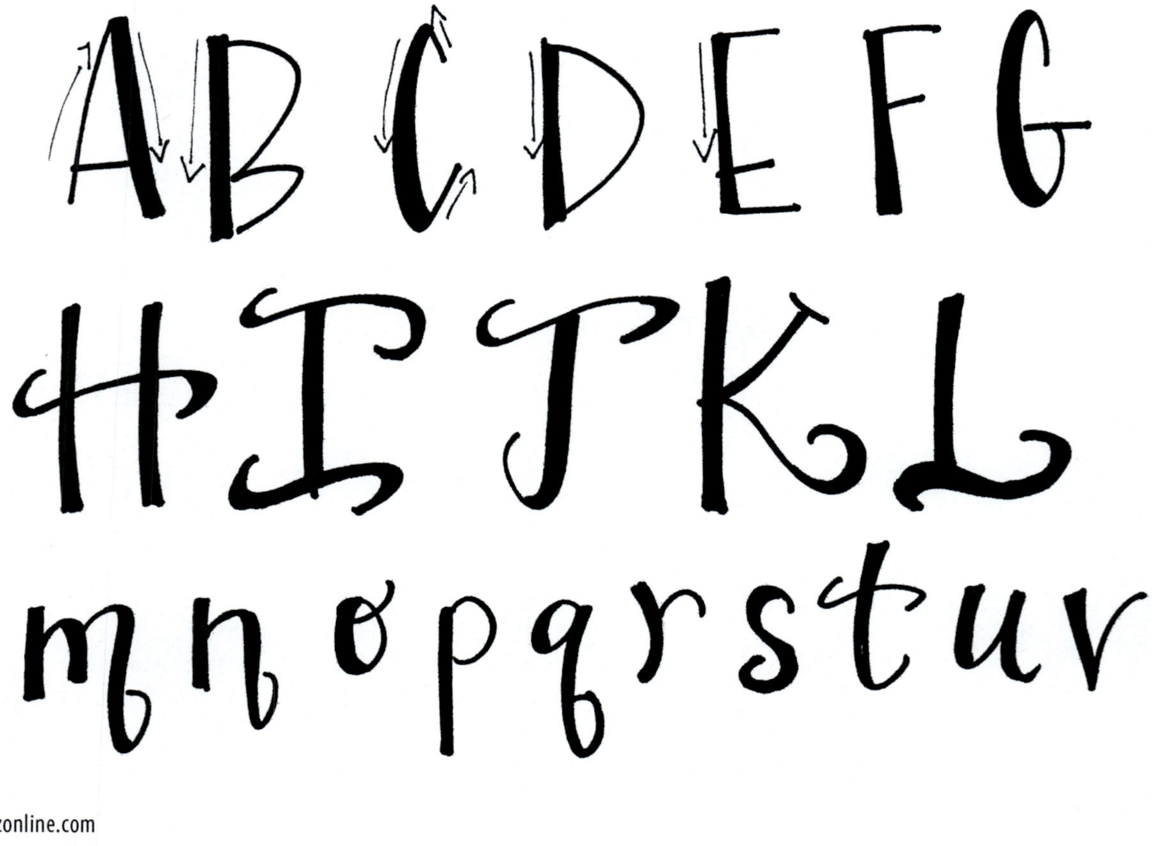

Practice here

HANDWRITING Technique

Tall & Skinny

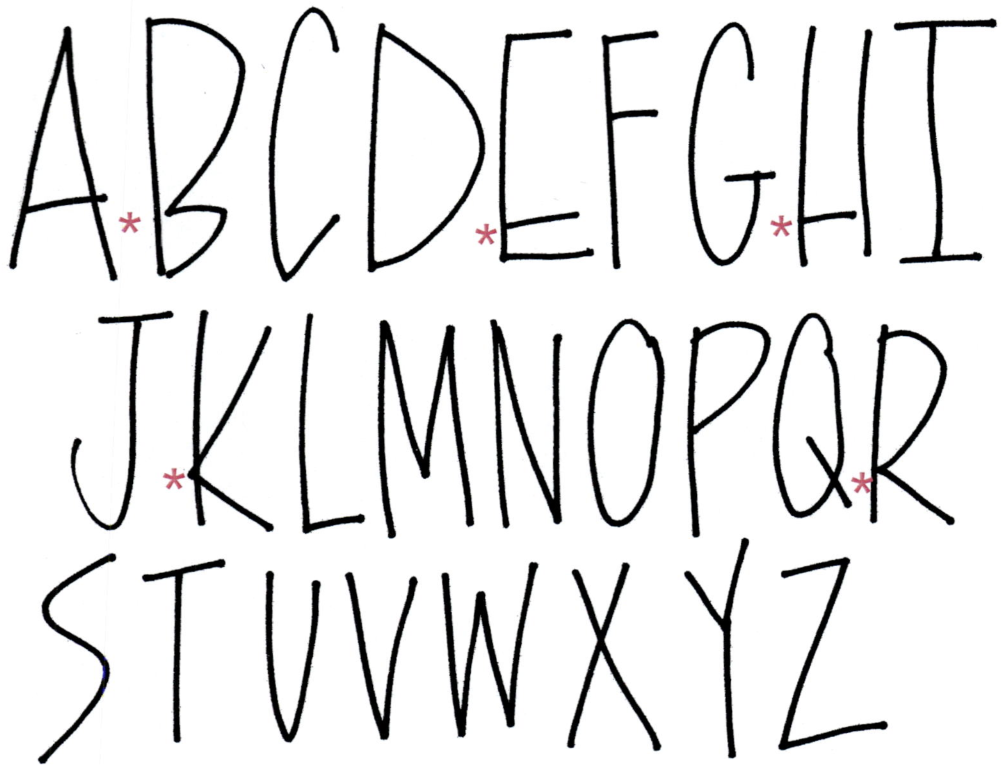

*Lower Cross Bars

Curls & Swirls

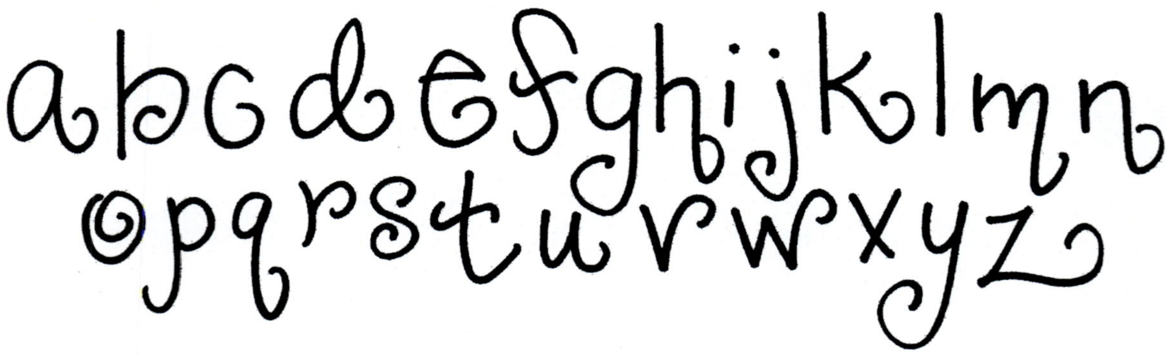

Practice here

ART Technique Watercolor Resist

SUPPLIES: Sharpie • White Oil Pastel • Watercolor

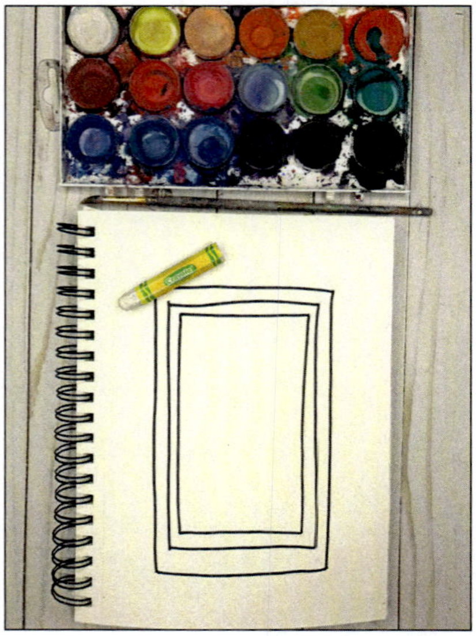

1 Draw several different sized rectangles.

2 Using pencil first, write out your verses.

3 Trace with Sharpie. Thicken up your downstrokes!

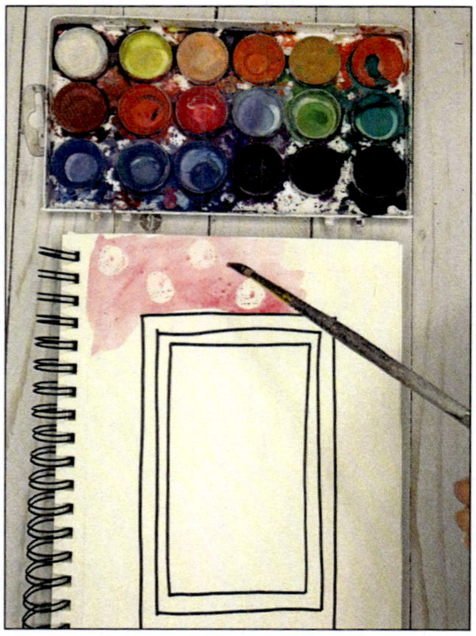

4 Using white oil pastel, add in your design.

5 Finally, fill with watercolor!

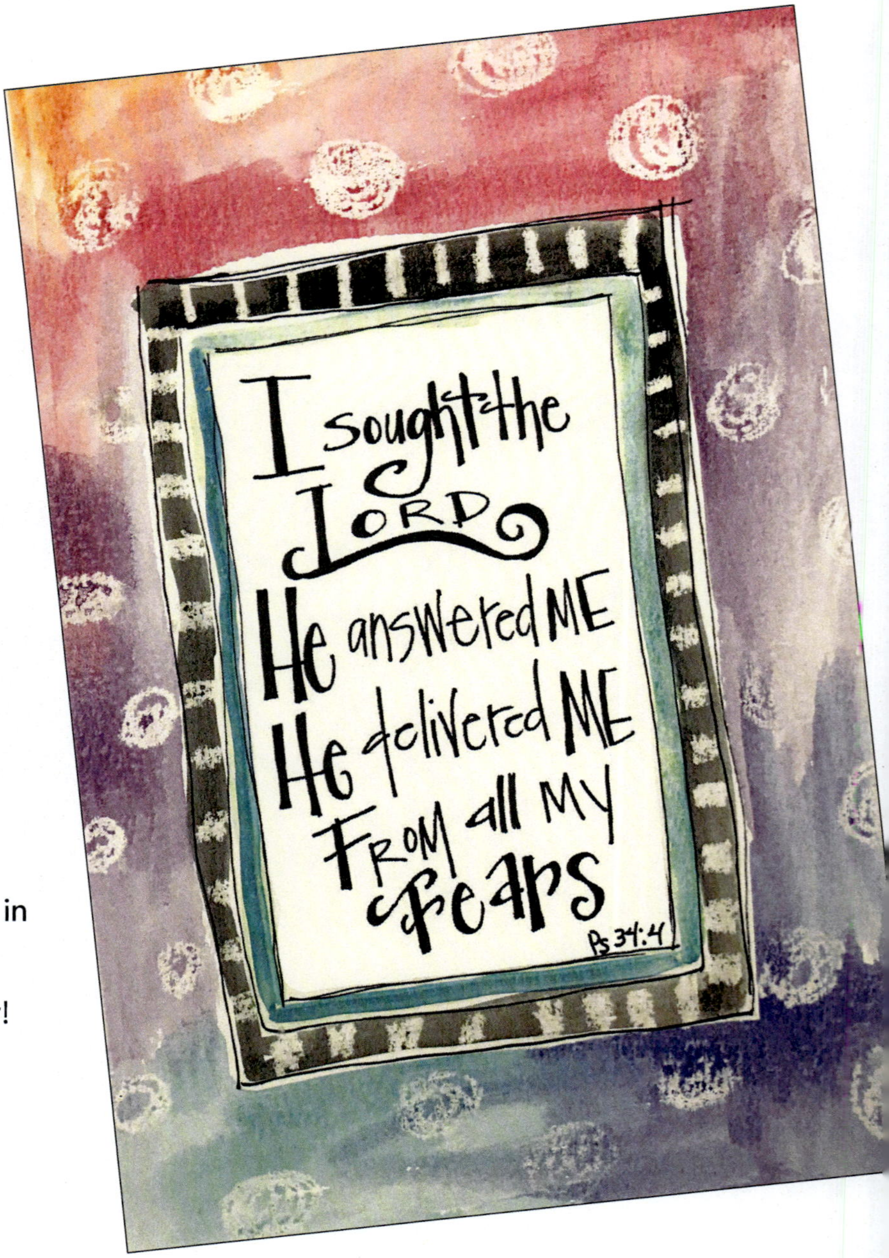

Practice Your Lettering Here

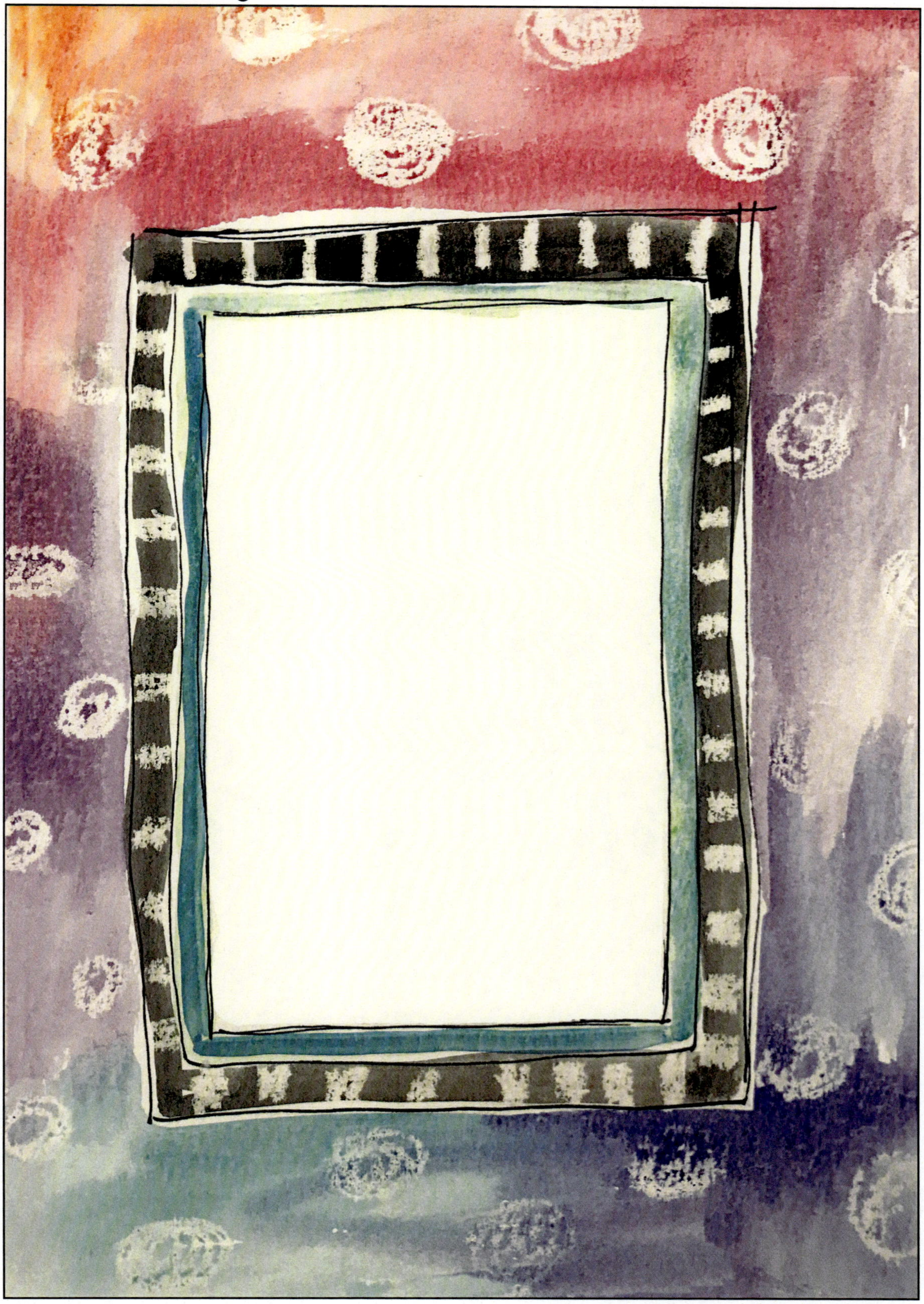

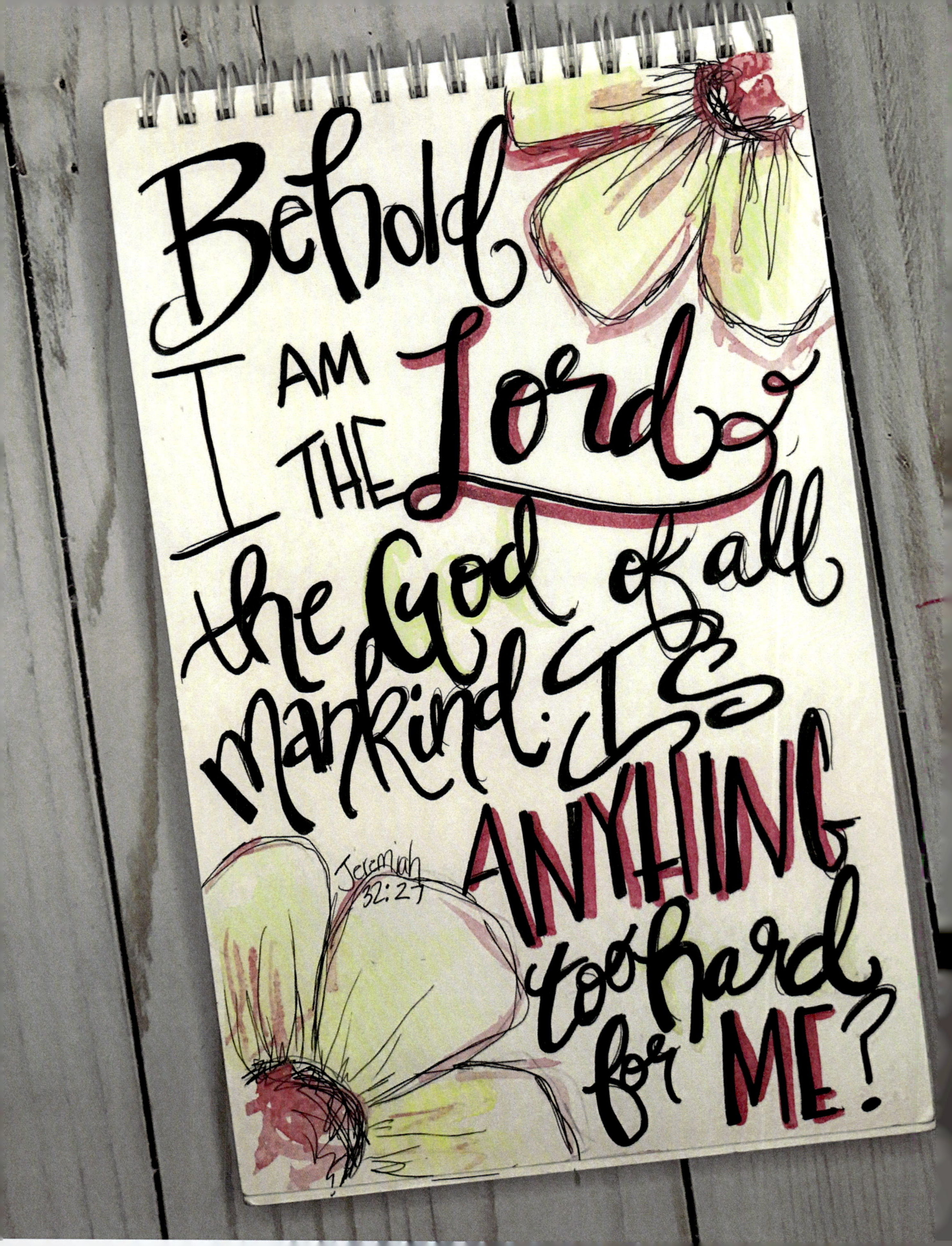
Behold
I AM THE Lord
the God of all mankind:
IS ANYTHING
too hard
for ME?
Jeremiah 32:27

Practice Your Lettering Here

Extra Practice

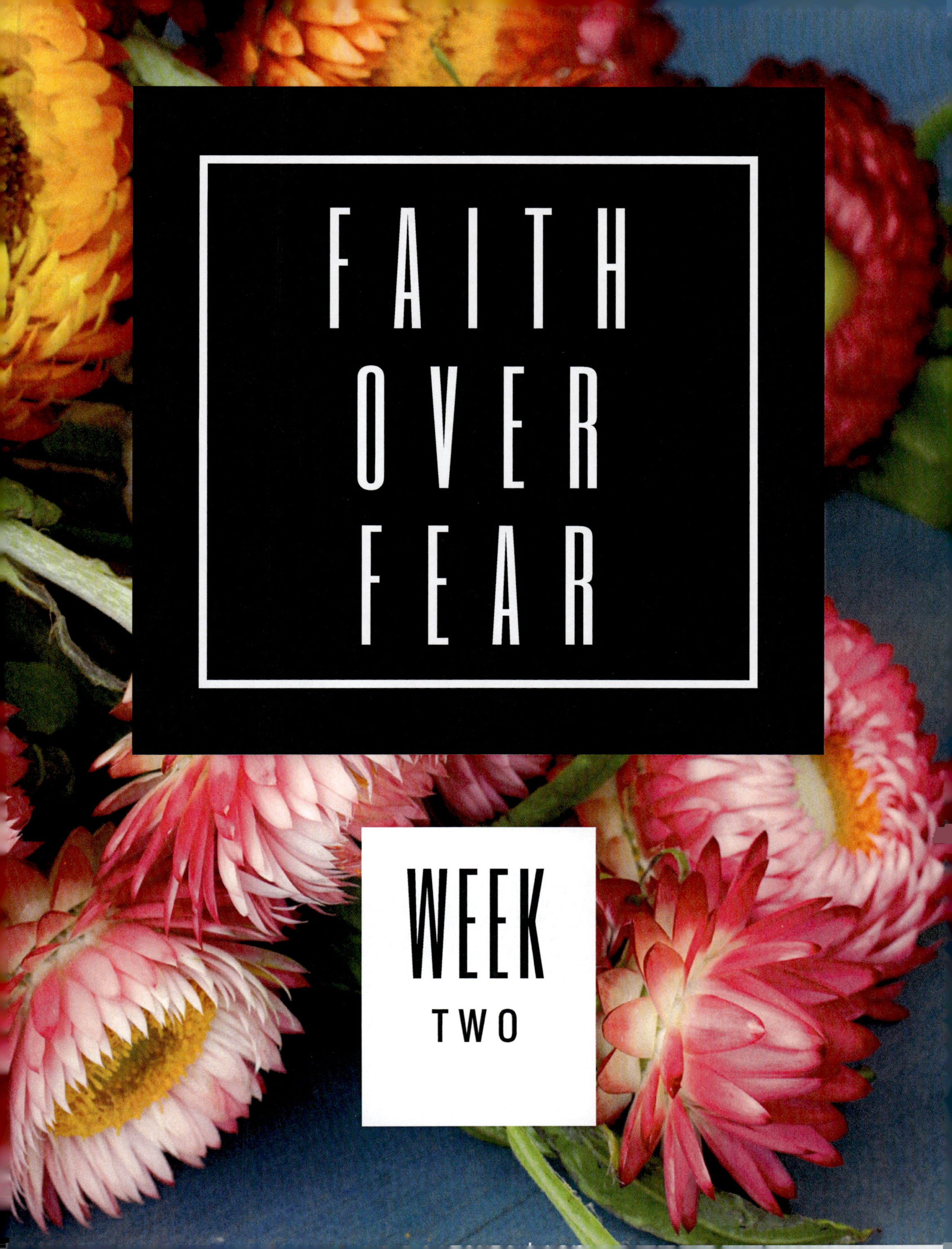

FAITH OVER FEAR

WEEK TWO

WEEK TWO: FEAR OF WHAT OTHERS THINK

A few weeks ago my son and I were walking through the parking lot of the local ball field. He had a baseball game and he looked so cute in his little baseball outfit. I just couldn't contain my words and I just said, "I love you so much! You are so cute and I just LOVE you. Do you know that!?"

When he looked at me, his first reaction was not one of thankfulness or appreciation. Oh no, he was horrified that I was saying this stuff out loud! With his eyes looking around to see who heard me, he quietly mumbled, "Mommm, be quiet! Somebody's gonna hear you!" I was like, "Who cares?! Nobody cares that I am saying this to you. I'm your mom for Pete's sake!" But in his little mind, he is still in that stage where he thinks that everybody is thinking something about him. And if they were to hear his mom talking like that, WHAT WOULD THEY THINK!?

I can clearly remember lots of times in grade school replaying things over and over in my head... wondering what people thought of me. It wasn't until I was a little bit older that I realized people don't really think about me too much.

[People are way too busy thinking about themselves to be thinking about me.]

However, even though we grow up and move past the grade-school obsession of what others think... often, we don't fully grow out of this fear. It may take on different forms as we grow older, but it's still there.

Some of the forms that this fear takes on is fear of rejection (what if they don't like me?); fear of failure (what if I try this and fail? I will look like an idiot. What will people think?); and fear of not being good enough (do they think I'm good enough?). All of these fears really narrow down to what other people think of us. You see, if we focus our mind more on what God thinks than what man thinks, we would remember... He isn't going to reject us, He can redeem any failure, and He knows we're not good enough, but that's why he sent Jesus!! His power is perfect in our weaknesses!!

How does the fear of what other people think play out in your life? In what areas of your life do you see this as problem? Feel free to discuss this with your group.

____

____

____

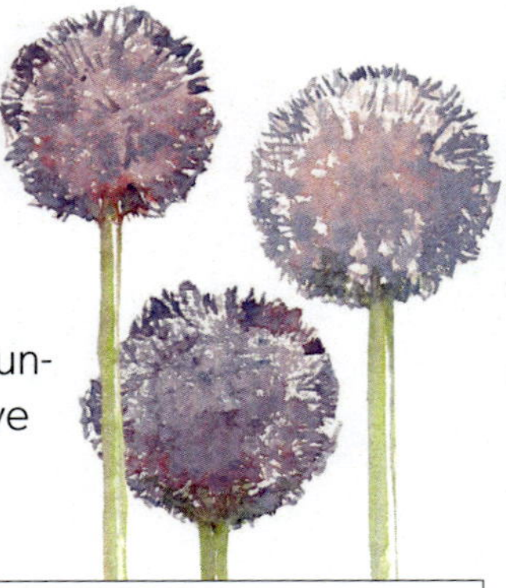

IN order to battle the thoughts and anxiety of what others think about us, we must start feeding our mind with God's Truth. *Honestly, feeding your mind with TRUTH is the remedy to help battle ANY fear!* We have got to consistently feed our minds with TRUTH.

Read TRUTH, memorize TRUTH, say it out loud during your day and over your life. While you are driving, speak these verses out loud. Just let it get deep inside of you until you believe these truths instead of the lies the enemy is trying to feed you. We have got to renew our minds. And that is gonna take some work. But we can do it!!

Proverbs 29:25 says, "Fear of man will prove to be a snare, but whoever trusts in the Lord is kept safe."

Craig Groshel says, "To obsess about what others think about us is the quickest way to forget what God thinks about us. BUT to obsess about what God thinks about us is the quickest way to forget what others think about us." Let's take a look at what Scripture tells us...

We are the Aroma of Christ

2 Corinthians 2:14 "But thanks be to God, who always leads us as captives in Christ's triumphal procession and uses us to spread the aroma of the knowledge of him everywhere."

I am a Child of God

John 1:12 "Yet to all who did receive him, to those who believed in his name, he gave the right to become children of God."

I am God's Co-Worker

1 Corinthians 3:9 "For we are co-workers in God's service; you are God's field, God's building."

God's Spirit Dwells in Me

1 Corinthians 3:16 "Don't you know that you yourselves are God's temple and that God's Spirit dwells in your midst?"

I am Valuable and Created in His Image

Genesis 1:27 "So God created man in His own image, in the image of God he created him male and female He created them."

Psalm 139:14 "I praise you because I am fearfully and wonderfully made: your works are wonderful, I know that full well."

Matthew 10:31 "So don't be afraid; you are worth more than many sparrows."

I am Forgiven

1 John 1:9 "If we confess our sins, he is faithful and just and will forgive us our sins and purify us from all unrighteousness."

I am Saved by Grace

Ephesians 2:8 "For it is by grace you have been saved, through faith and this is not from yourselves, it is the gift of God."

God will Never Leave Me

Hebrews 13:5 "Keep your lives free from the love of money and be content with what you have, because God has said, 'Never will I leave you; never will I forsake you.' "

Search the scriptures for what God thinks about us and who He says we are! Write your own here. We will use these to write and watercolor our art this week.

1 ______________________________

2 ______________________________

3 ______________________________

4 ______________________________

5 ______________________________

6 ______________________________

I challenge you to take a verse and commit it to memory this week! My favorite way to memorize scripture is to put it to a beat or a song. Even if it's silly, make up a little beat and memorize God's Truth. This is the hard work that's gonna help us renew our minds and fill our mind with Truth. You can do it!!

HANDWRITING Technique
Swap Up Styles

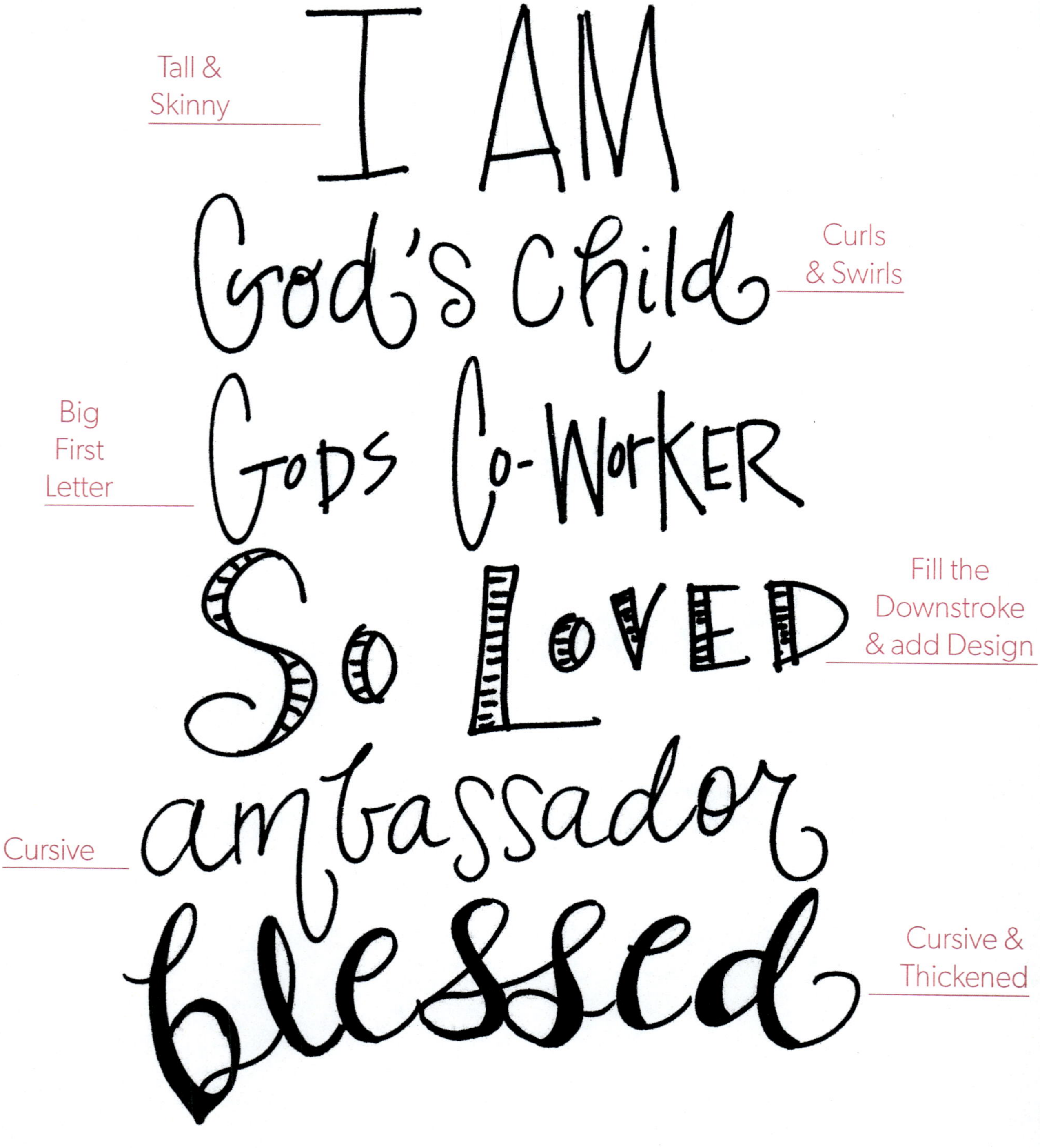

Practice here

HANDWRITING Technique
More Swapping Fonts

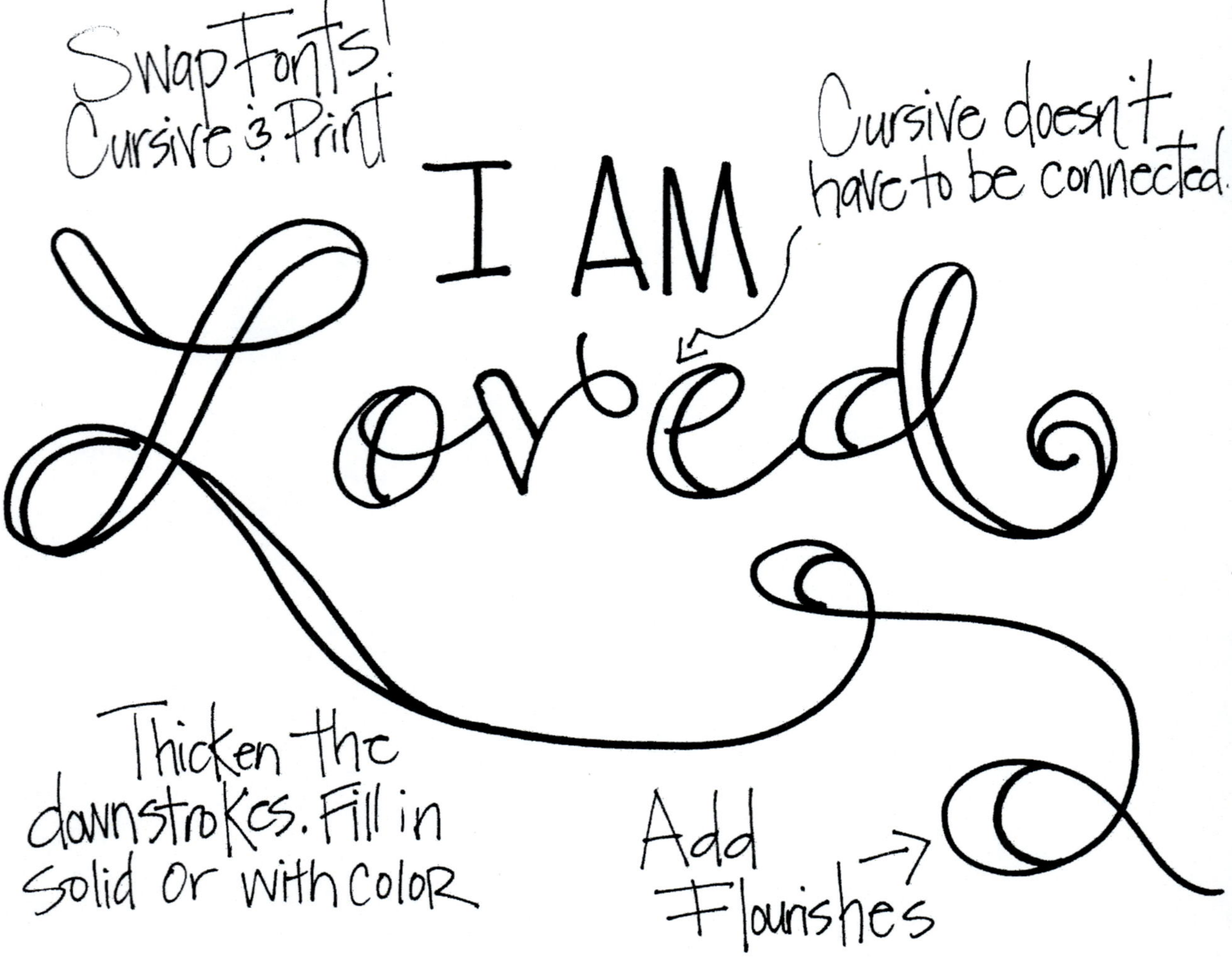

Practice here

ART Technique Lifting Off

SUPPLIES:

Watercolor Paper • Watercolor • Paper Towel • Pencil • Sharpie

1 Draw a horizon line and paint sky with loose wet color.

2 Use a paper towel to "lift off" some areas for clouds.

3 Paint sandbar with scribbly hand.

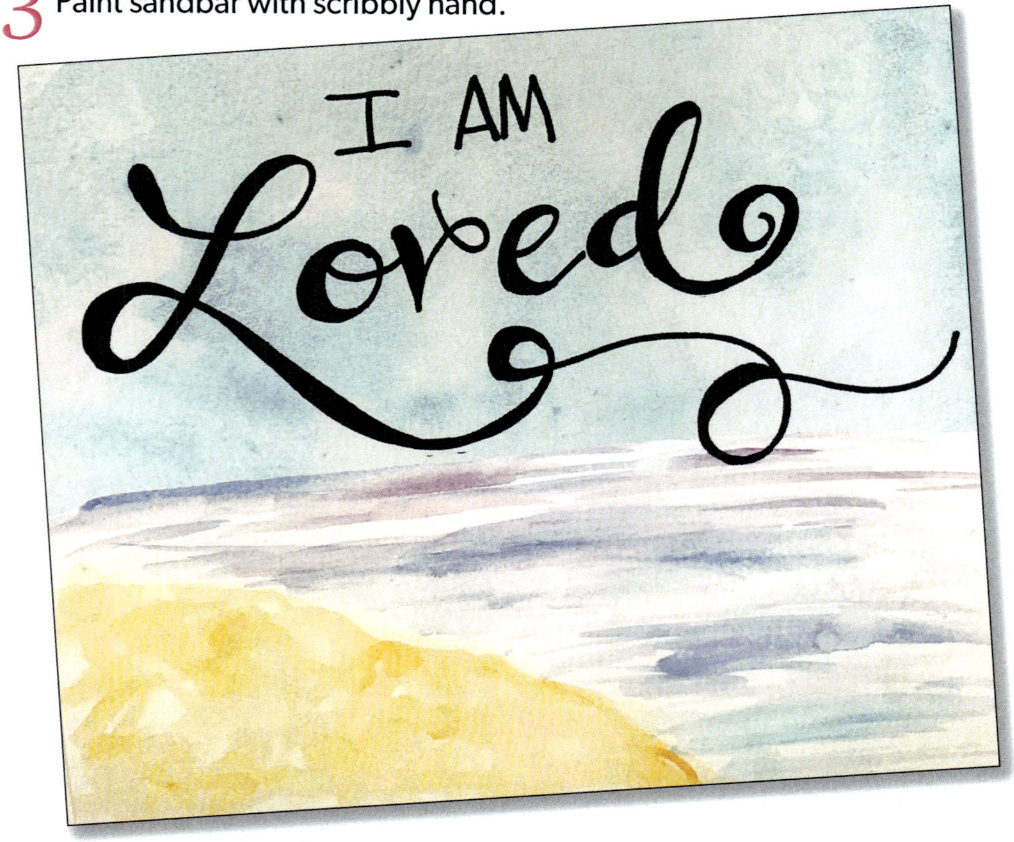

4 Using side-to-side strokes and multiple colors, add in your water. Be sure to leave some white spaces too.

5 Once the painting has dried, you can pencil in your lettering.

6 Then finalize your lettering with Sharpie!

TIP! For more detailed instruction, watch the video at www.pzazzonline.com!

Practice Your Lettering Here

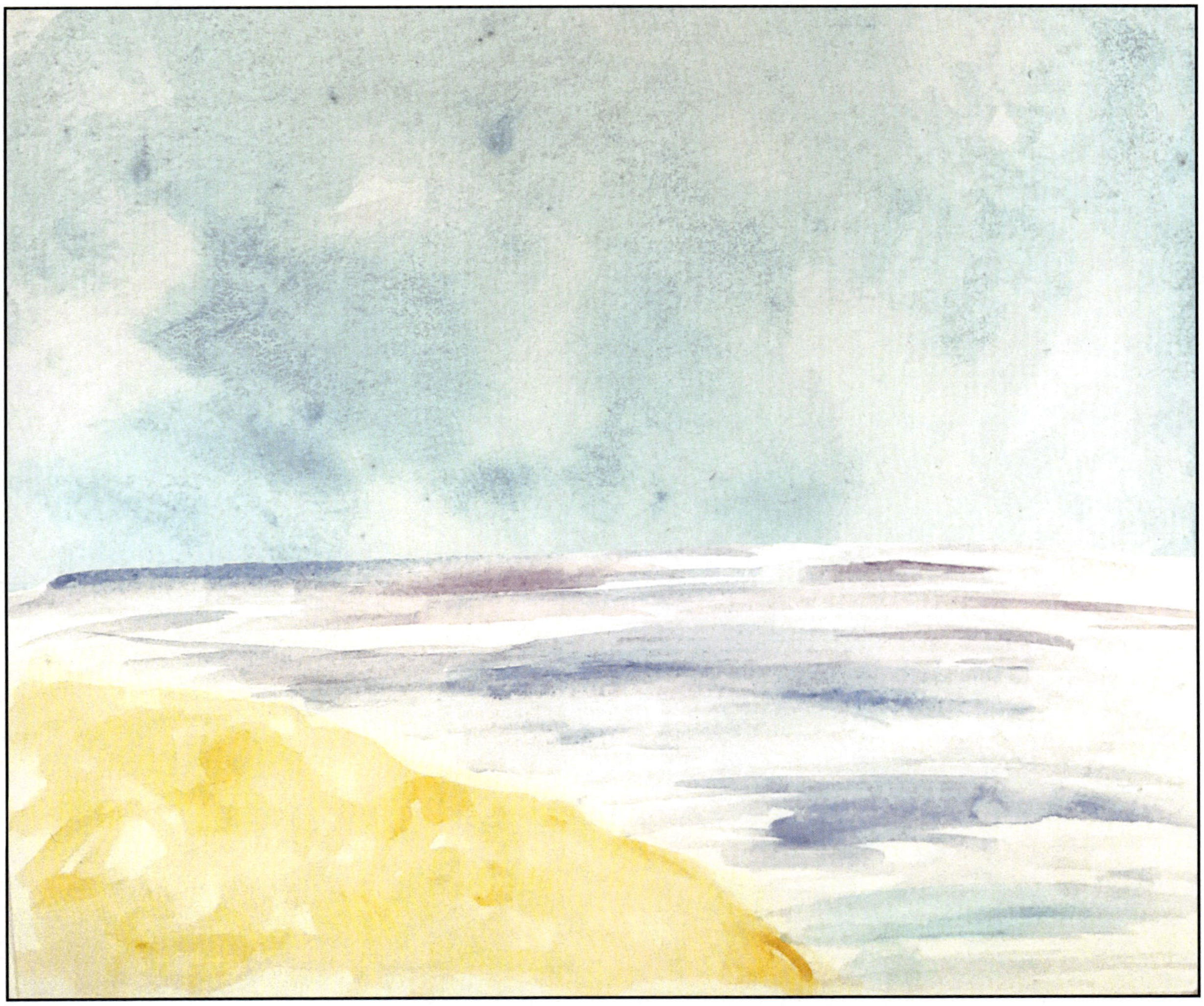

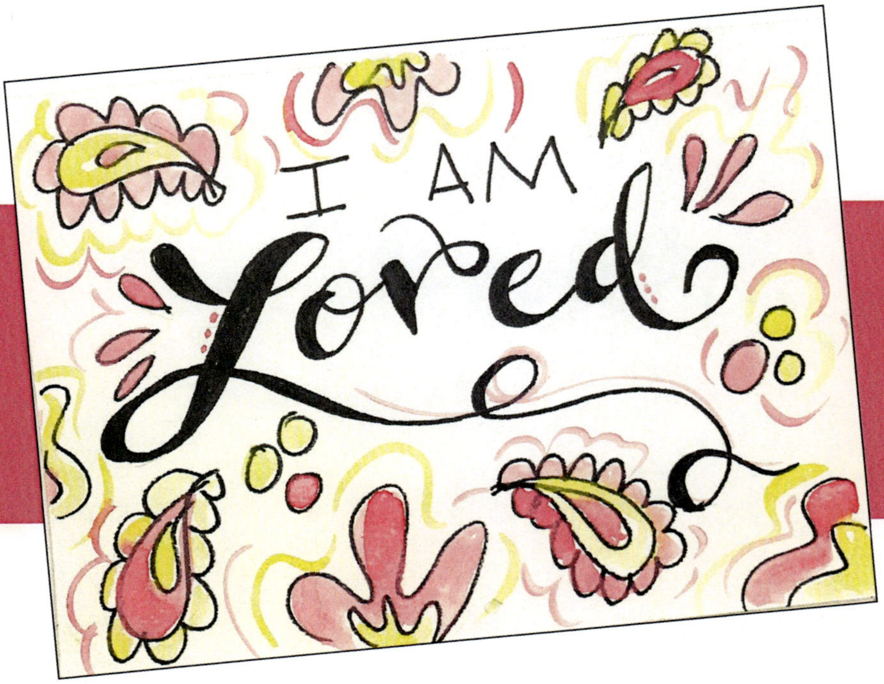

Here is another layout idea for this lettering! Be creative and have some fun!

ART Technique Wet-on-Wet Watercolor

SUPPLIES: Watercolor Paper • Watercolor • Pencil • Sharpie

1 Pencil in your lettering and border.

2 Trace with sharpie and erase leftover pencil marks. Thicken the letters that you want to be thicker.

3 Wet your paper with plain water first. Do this one small section at a time. In this case, it's the section inside our border.

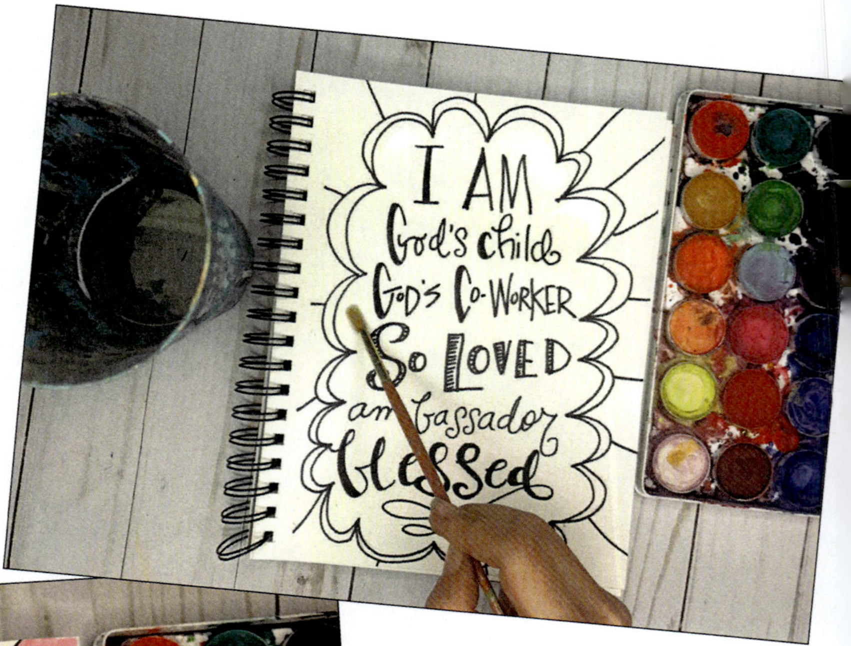

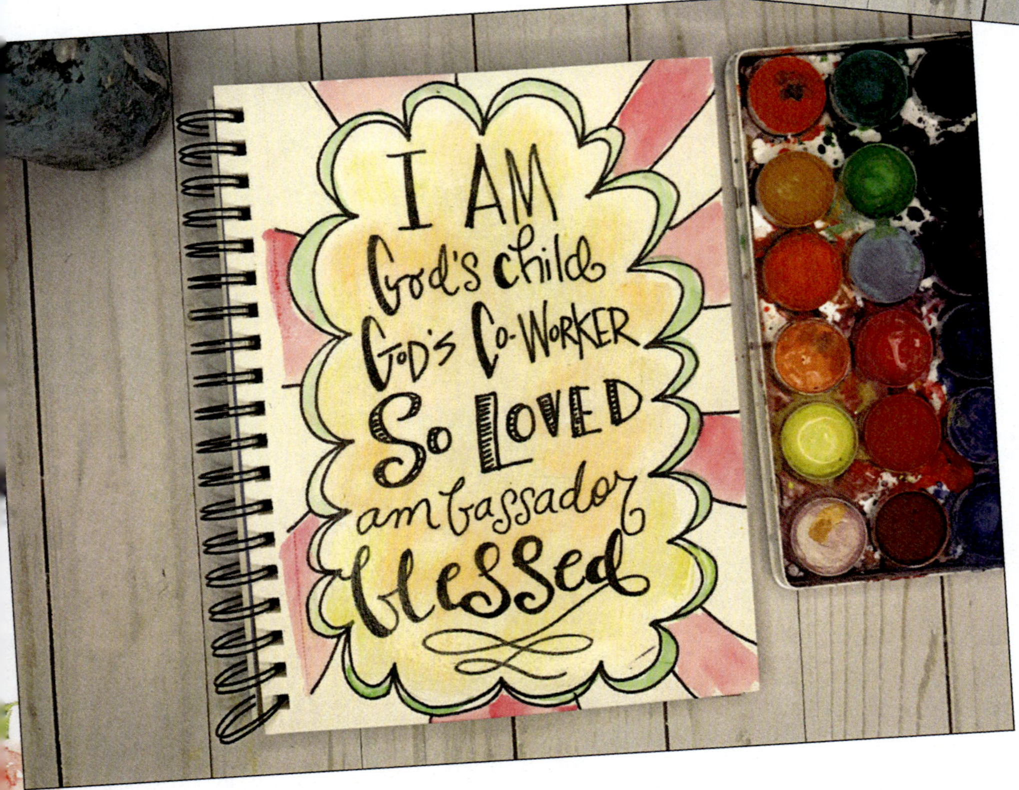

4 While it's still wet, begin dropping in colors. Here we used yellow and orange. You should start to see a cool tie-dye effect with this wet-on-wet technique.

5 Paint the rest of your picture with watercolors. No special technique required!

There you have it! A cool painting that reminds you who you are in Christ!! Now don't forget it! Put this somewhere that you will see it all week!!

Practice Your Lettering Here

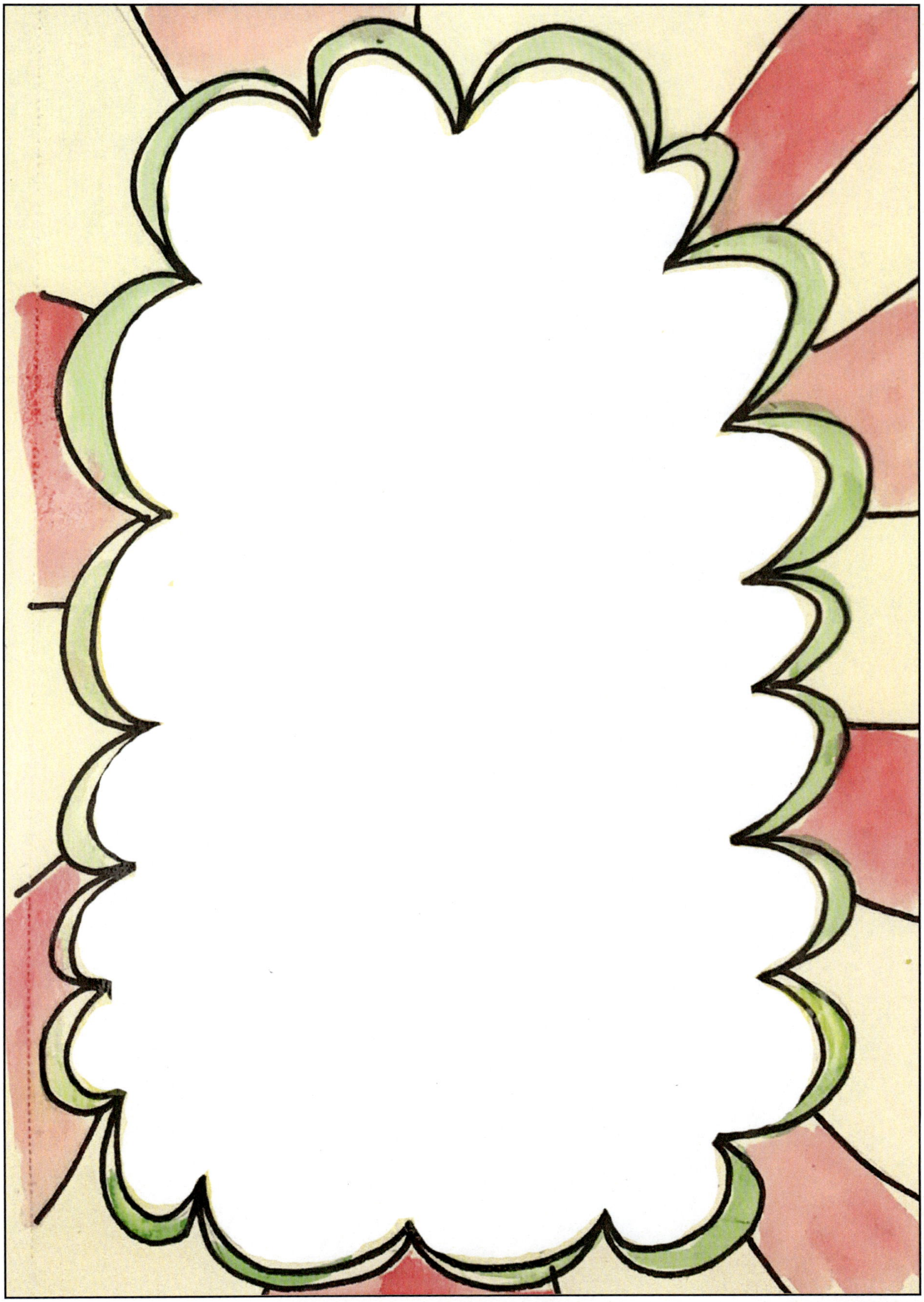

Extra Practice

FAITH OVER FEAR

WEEK THREE

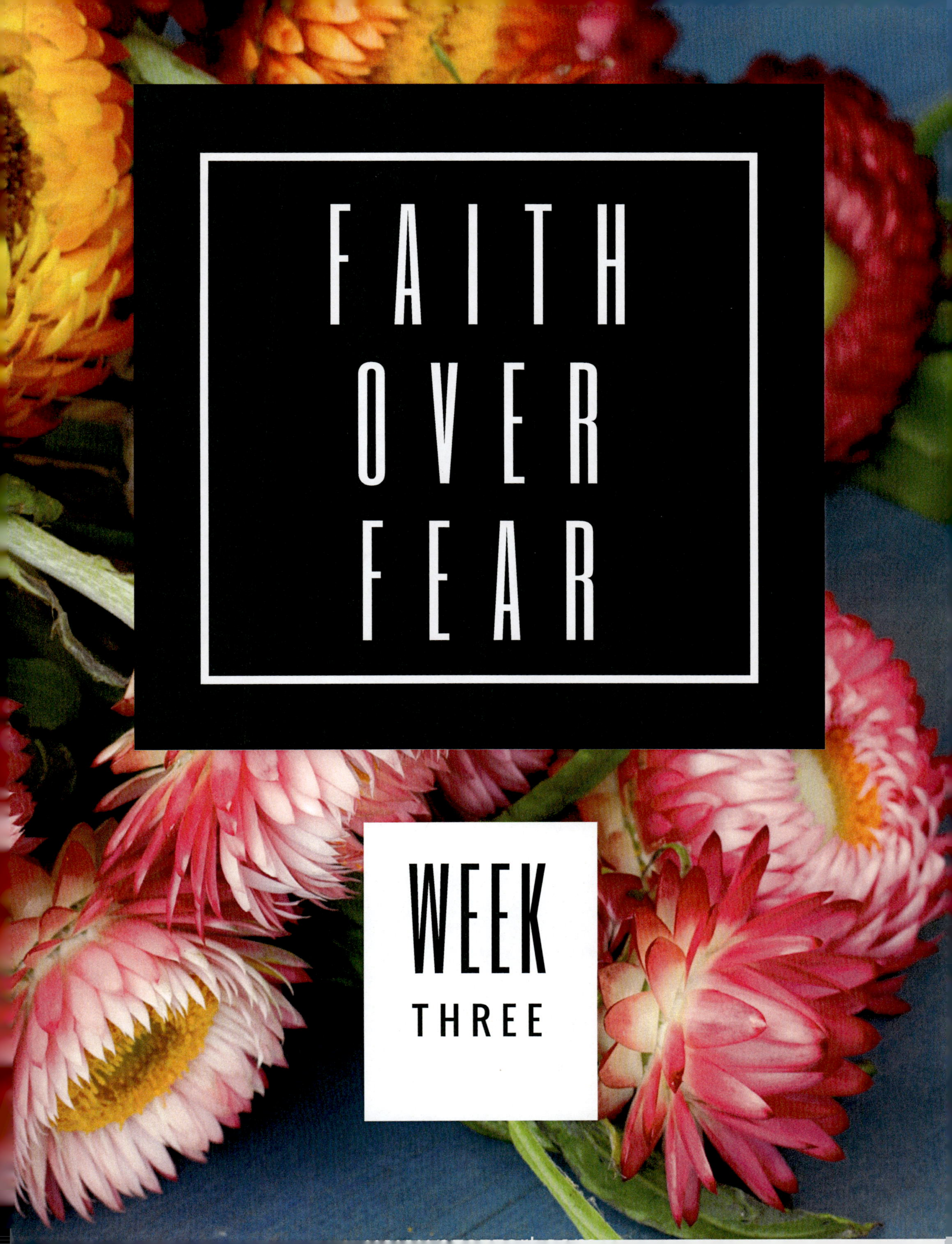

WEEK THREE: FEAR OF NOT HAVING ENOUGH

How's it going y'all?!

Have you memorized any of the verses you've been journaling? **Ok, pop quiz!** Take some time to share them in your group now. If you need to look over them real quick, that's fine. But say these out loud to your group or if you are doing this alone, say it out loud to yourself! Keep yourself accountable. Renewing your mind takes work. It takes time to memorize these scriptures. It takes faith to believe these scriptures are true. You got this. Ok, so say your verses from memory... Go!

Years ago, I had a business coach that worked with me to keep me in my best state. What I mean by that is that at my best I was patient, energetic, creative, inspiring and fun. But then other times I was sooooo not patient; I was snappy, aggravated, stressed, overwhelmed, and anxious. We did some practical things to deal with the issues that were causing stress, but we also did some mind work.

It sounds a little crazy but she asked me to write down all the qualities of me at my "best self." Even some qualities that didn't describe me, but I wanted them to. I wrote them down. Then she said, "Now put them in your notes on your phone. I want you to look at this list and say it out loud 7-10 times each day. When you stop at a red light, look at them and say them. When you first get up, look at it and say them."

"All day long, have little triggers to remind yourself who you are at your best self."

Ok, I know it seems a little strange to do that, but the point was to renew my mind. I wasn't allowing my mind to become "Stressed Out Kasey"... I was conditioning it to stay in the "Creative, Kind, Kasey Mode." I paid this business coach some big bucks to basically tell me the same thing that the Bible already tells us for free. RENEW YOUR MIND!!

So what does this story have to do with today's lesson... well, not much. But it has everything to do with the point that ***it takes work***. Please don't let these weekly lessons be the only time you are in your Bible. Don't let this be the only time you are reading these verses. Meditate on them day and night. Put them in your phone and look at them 7 times a day... at a stop light, when you first wake up, before you go to bed.

Do the work and invite the Holy Spirit in to do what only He can do, and y'all I promise... it's gonna make all the difference in the world! Fears can be gone. Stress and anxiety can slowly become a thing of the past. Fear is not something that has to be in your life! Access the gift of the Holy Spirit and let's get this thing gone!!

With all this Holy Spirit talk, now would also be a good time to note... The Holy Spirit is available to all when you believe in Jesus Christ as God's son, your Savior, and Lord of your life. Ephesians 1:13 "And you also were included in Christ when you heard the message of truth, the gospel of your salvation. When you believed, you were marked in him with a seal, the promised Holy Spirit...." So when you hear me talking about the Holy Spirit and his power, please understand, everybody can have access to the Holy Spirit through Christ. However, that doesn't mean that everybody does have access to the Holy Spirit. You have to take that step in faith and believe in Jesus! And then y'all, life gets so fun!

Ok, so let's get to today's discussion: *the fear of not having enough.*

Do y'all face this? Because this is something that has plagued me for years. I honestly don't know how I've made it 10 years being an entrepreneur. When you are in business for yourself, you have no idea how much money is coming in. I guess the fear drives me sometimes, but the fear has always been there.

I have always thought, "Will we have enough? Will my business bring in enough money to cover the bills and for us to eat? What if something big pops up and I don't have the resources to cover it?"

There were so many "what if's" that were constantly in my mind. And it went beyond money. "What if my ideas dry up? My business is based on my creative ideas, my paintings, my events, my classes... what if one day I can't think of any more ideas?" I just had an overall fear of running out of resources; whether that be money, creativity, ideas, etc.

Can you relate? In what ways to do you fear not having enough?

It's hard to hear sometimes, but it's true... the areas you fear the most are where you are trusting God the least. Let me say that again.

Where we fear the most is where we trust God the least!

Yikes. When that reality hit me, I was like, "Ok, God. I want to trust you with this area. Show me how." So He took me on a little journey through the Bible. I began researching and listening to sermons on what God says about money. Glance over at Exodus 16. Do you see the story of the manna and the quail? If you aren't familiar with it, read over it.

Basically, the Lord rained down food from heaven. He took care of their most basic need in a miraculous way. He did this day after day for 40 years!! Next look at Exodus 16:4. "Then the Lord said to Moses, 'I will rain down bread from heaven for you. The people are to go out each day and gather enough for that day. In this way I will test them and see whether they will follow my instructions." He completely provided. But he had some conditions.

He wanted them to follow some instructions to see if they really trusted Him. In this case the instructions were ***1) only take what you need for that day and don't save any for the next day.*** The ones who didn't follow this instruction and saved some for the morning... their food was full of maggots and began to smell. His other instruction: ***2) gather twice as much as they needed on the 6th day and save it for the 7th day.*** The 7th day was the Sabbath, a day of rest and worship. (Even so, some people still went out on the 7th day looking for food and there was none).

Now God could have easily made the food so it wouldn't rot or He could have provided food on the Sabbath. The point is that He had some guidelines in place to test the people. He wanted to see how much they believed Him.

He wanted to give them an opportunity to grow their faith and watch Him work.

And we know that faith is what pleases God. Hebrews 11:6: "Without faith it is impossible to please God." So these guidelines aren't in place to keep us from something good. They are in place to give us an opportunity to see God show up!!

So, ok. They had those guidelines... but we don't have manna and quail, so how does this apply to us? Well, we have guidelines with our money as well. I could spend a lot of time talking about what Jesus says about money. But today we are going to focus on just one guideline. Because I believe this one guideline is the hardest for so many of us. And if we aren't getting it right, then we aren't fully seeing God show up.

Let's explore these verses. Look them up and write them here. If you have any questions, write those down too. You may want to discuss those in your small group.

Proverbs 3:9-10 ______________________________

Proverbs 11:25 ______________________________

Malachi 3:8-10 ______________________________

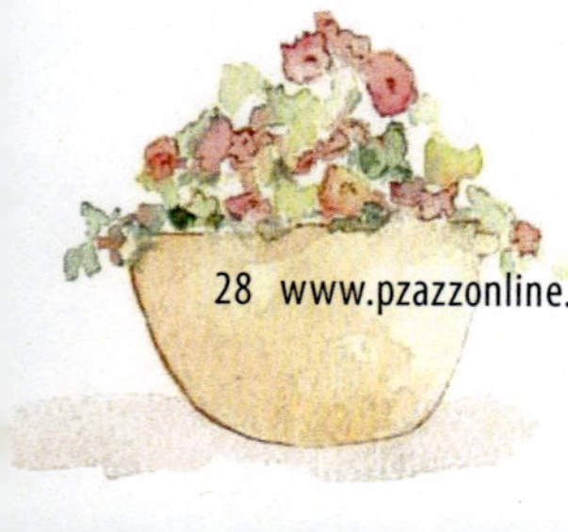

What do these verses mean to you? What do they make clear?

To me, these verses make 3 things clear.

God honors generosity. ***Psalm 41:1-3***

He is a giver and He wants us to be like Him. He wants us to be generous and to give!!

God commands a tithe. ***Malachi 3:10-12***

A tithe literally means tenth, so in our culture that is 10% of your paycheck. And He also PROMISES to bless the tithe! He says, "Test me in this!" If you aren't quite sure about doing money God's way... then test Him! He asks you to. He says, test me in giving your tithe and just see if I don't provide. Y'all, He does. I've seen it time and time again.

Provision doesn't always come in the form of money. Sometimes it comes by way of someone else buying you a meal or if you watched the video from this week... provision may come in the form of a banana tree. Someway, somehow, God always provides when we are following His commands.

Not only does God want us to give a tithe back to the local church, but he wants our firstfruits. ***Proverbs 3:9***

That means tithe at the beginning of the month, or as soon as you get paid. Proverbs 3:9 says to honor God with your firstfruits! You see, if you tithe at the end of the month, that's not really tithing on faith. That's tithing because you know you have it. When you give at the beginning of the month, it's on faith because you don't know what may come up. In some cases you may not even know what may come in. You are giving to God on faith. Because remember... faith is what pleases God and when you give on faith, you get the extraordinary blessing of seeing God provide!

Now at this point you may be like, "Hold up... I was fearful of running out of resources before I started this study... and now you are telling me to give money away... say what???"

I hear ya! It doesn't seem like it makes sense. But the thing is... once you see God provide once, then you trust him with the tithe the next month and you see Him provide, and then you do it again and again. What starts to happen is that you see that God is always faithful and He has unlimited resources. Money is not an issue with Him. It's our heart that He wants to work on. The more you see Him provide, the more you trust him. This builds your faith. So you see, these guidelines are put into place to give us a chance to see God work!!

Please don't hear this as saying that if you tithe... you "GET" something in return. If you tithe like that, then your heart still isn't where God wants it to be. God wants to work greed and selfishness OUT OF US and when we tithe with the right attitude, that's exactly what it does. We can't be selfish when we are giving our money away. We are not being "greedy" when we are learning to give. But if we have the "GIVE TO GET" mentality, well... that works greed and selfishness right back into our heart. And that is not what God wants.

So I challenge you. If you aren't tithing, start. And if maybe you are like me and you tithe, but not always at the beginning of the month... then start that. God wants our firstfruits! He wants to build our faith. Learning to trust Him with our money is how we lose the fear of not having enough!!

What are you going to do this week to follow what God says about money?

HANDWRITING Technique

Hollow Letters

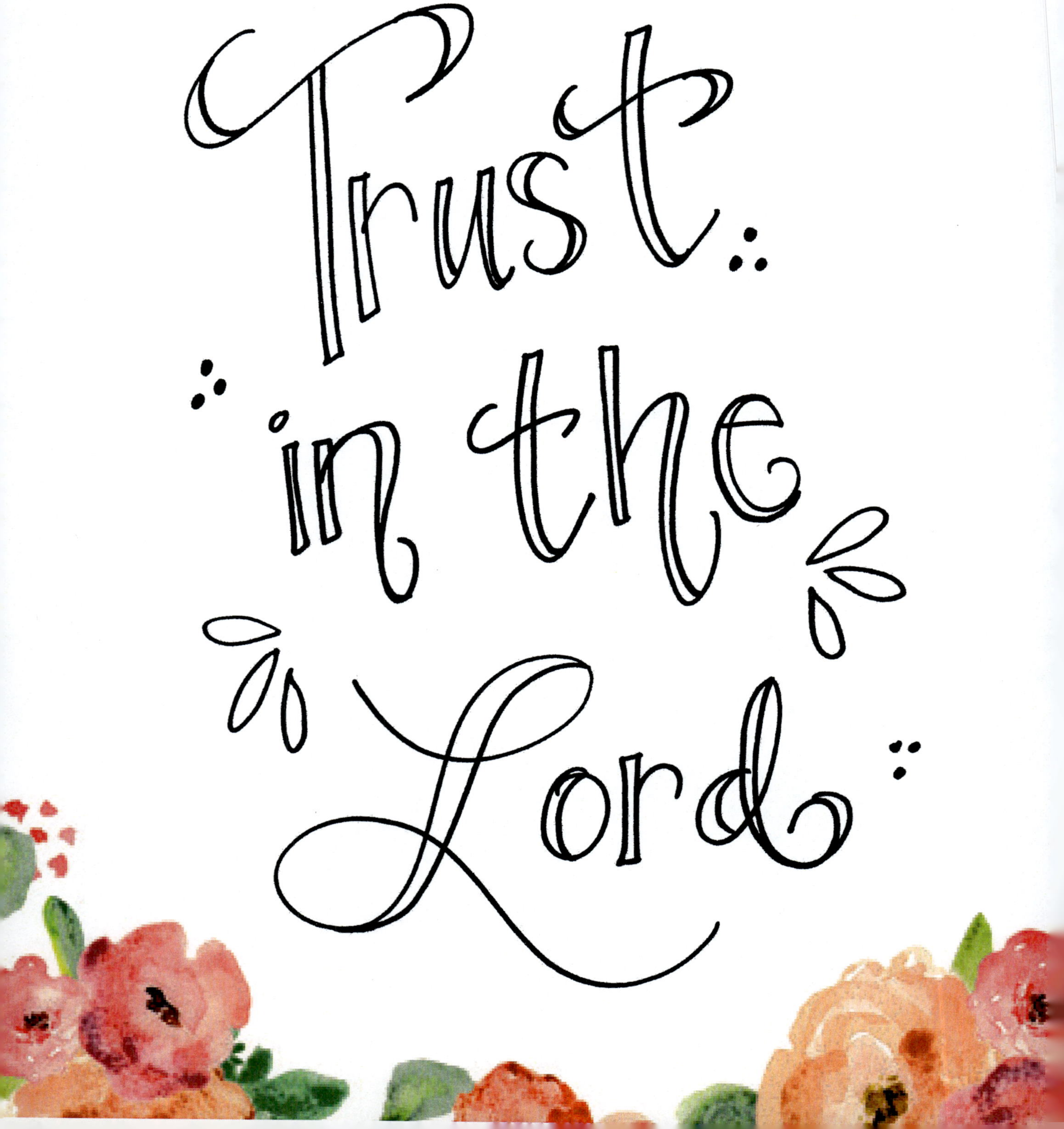

Practice here

ART Technique Painting Watercolor Roses

SUPPLIES: Pan Watercolors • Watercolor Paper • Sharpie • Pencil
Small Watercolor Brush • Water

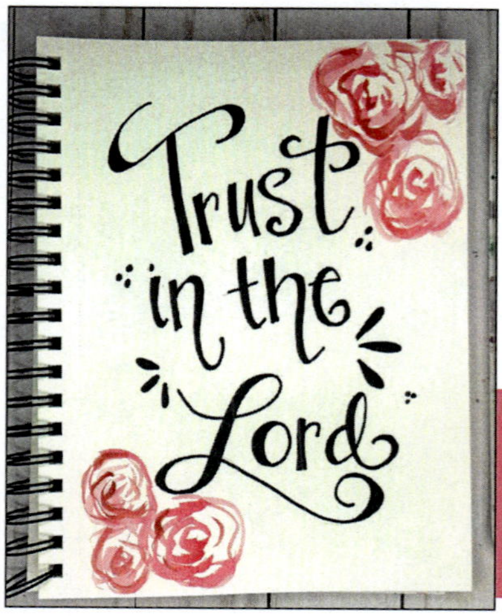

1 With a small brush and some pink, lightly draw out where your roses will go. These should be loose circle type shapes, but NOT perfect circles.

2 Next, begin placing in some loose squiggly C-type lines on the left side of the circles.

Watch this technique demonstrated on the companion video! (www.pzazzonline.com)

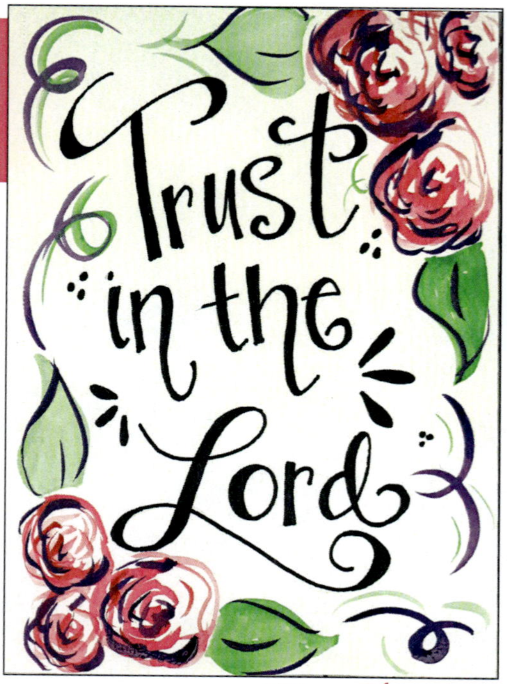

Proverbs 3:5-6

3 After that, layer in some pink and maybe some red primarily on the left side. Put a few loose backwards C's on the right side of the roses. Leave white space on the right side.

4 While waiting on the roses to dry, add in your green leaves.

5 Once everything is dry, use a small brush and dark purple to add definition and swirls. Be sure to put the purple primarily on the left side of the flowers!

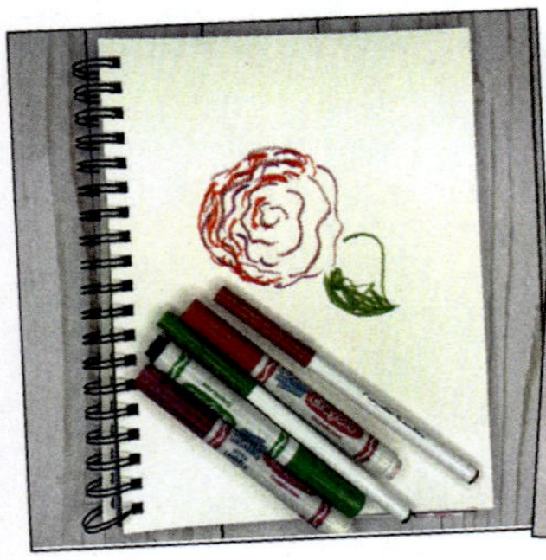
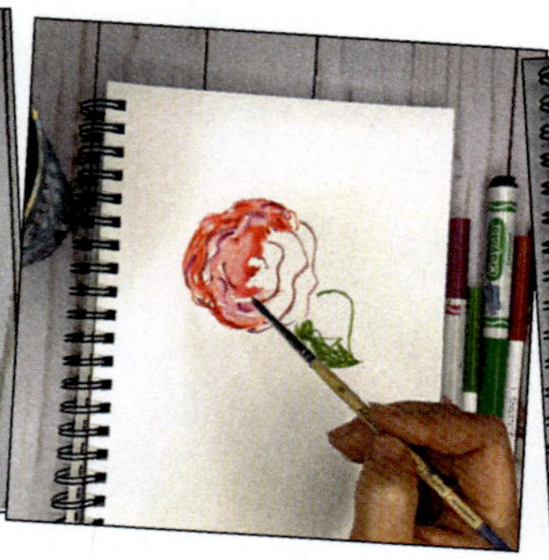
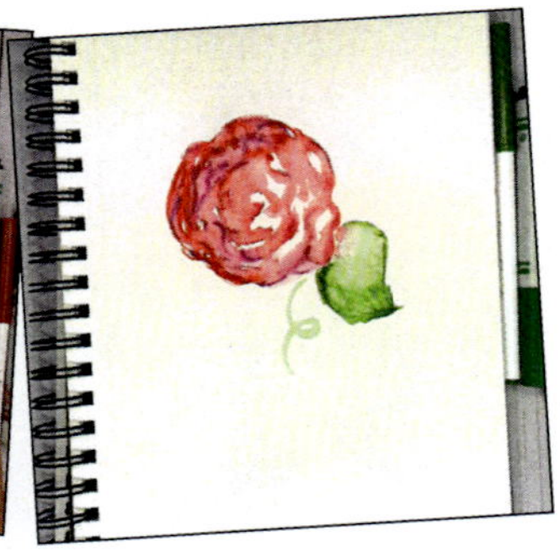

Bonus! Marker-to-Watercolor Technique

You can use washable markers to get fun water-color effects too!!

1 Simply use your marker to draw your flower.

2 Then add water with a watercolor brush! Voila! You've got a cool watercolor flower! Once again, be sure to leave some white space on the right side of the flower for a highlight!

Practice Your Lettering Here

Extra Practice

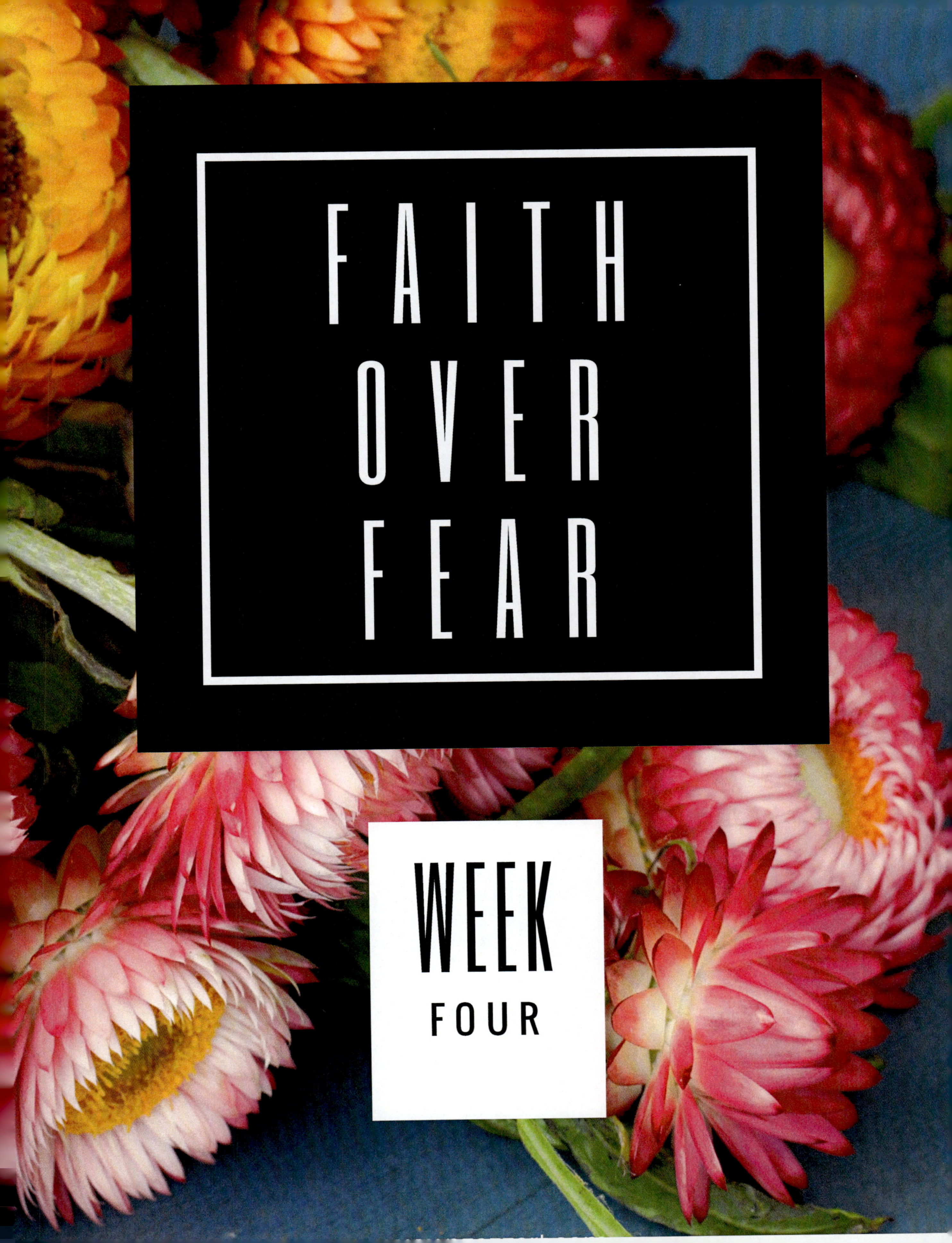

FAITH OVER FEAR

WEEK FOUR

WEEK FOUR: FEAR OF LOSING SOMEONE

Man, this is a hard one to write about. The thought of losing someone I love is almost too much to bear. Sometimes when I allow my mind to wander down the path of what could happen and how I would feel afterwards, I just sit there and cry.

I LOVE my people. My husband, my kids, my parents, my best friends. I love love love them. I see so many people in my life who have lost their children, their parents, their siblings, and although I have not gone through that… my heart hurts deeply.

This past summer, we were in Honduras at one the orphanages we help support through "Rice Bowls" (www.ricebowls.org). We asked people to donate items for us to distribute to the kids and the community. We packed them in these big duffle bags to get them overseas, and then once we got there and settled in, we unpacked the duffle bags and begin sorting the items: one pile of rice, one pile of socks, one pile of toothbrushes, etc. I noticed a big trash bag of clothes. I figured someone had donated old clothes. I wasn't sure what to do with them. About that moment, Johnny, our fearless leader, told me that a couple from the states had lost a son earlier that year. They wanted to donate his clothes to the orphanage. My job was to go through and begin sorting the clothes. Even as I write this, tears fill my eyes. I could not handle this assignment. He told me to sort the clothes but as I picked up these sweet little boy pajamas and realized a family had lost the little boy who used to wear those pajamas, I just couldn't do it.

Tears filled my eyes, my face got hot, and an overwhelming sense that I could barely breathe set in.

I quickly walked back to my room. I had to get away from everyone else because I was an emotional wreck. Everybody else was busy sorting items, but this bag… this bag was too hard. I sat in my room and just cried and tried to compose myself before going back out to the front porch. I honestly can't remember if I finished the job or if my sweet friend ended up doing it for me when she saw how it affected me. All I remember is that I felt that family's pain. In the same moment it hit hard to realize that this is one of my biggest fears.

Here's the deal… the reason it's so scary is because it's so real. People lose people everyday. I've seen it over and over.

One of my precious art students had an aunt Rhonda. Rhonda was young and beautiful. She had one little girl and one on the way. During her pregnancy she noticed a big lump on the side of her neck. Over time it was revealed that the lump was a very rare form of cancer. They ended up taking her baby early so she could begin treatment.

Rhonda was such a woman of faith, as is her whole family. When I say the community rallied around her… well, I have never seen so much support for one individual. Her Facebook page "A Living Hope" had over 20,000 members, t-shirts were made, billboards around town reminded people to pray for her. This town prayed and prayed for a miracle and for her healing. Ultimately, she wasn't healed on this earth. That prayer didn't get answered the way we'd hoped. But so many other prayers along the way did. But that big one didn't. And we just ask, "Why?"

If you haven't already, please watch this week's video. I sit down with Rhonda's sister, Robyn. Robyn shares such wisdom. She reminds us that to think this world is going be perfect is a false sense of entitlement. Heaven is a perfect place, but this earth is not. When sin entered this world, so did death and disease. In fact, the Bible tells us to expect trials.

John 16:33: "I have said these things to you, that in me you may have peace. In the world you will have tribulation. But take heart: I have overcome the world."

At one of the prayer vigils, Rhonda came in and stood at the front of the church. Part of the time, people just called out in prayer over her. And then she spoke up. She looked weak. Her hair was gone. She didn't look like herself at all. But her words were so powerful. She prayed to God and said something to the effect of "God, this is not my will. I want to be with my little girls and raise them. But God, I know that if I could see things the way you see them and know the things you know, then I would make the same decision that you are going to make." Essentially she was saying "Not my will but yours." I have to ask myself... am I at the point where I can say that? Are you? Can we truly say, "Not my will but yours, Father."

"God, I know that if I could see things the way you see them and know the things you know, then I would make the same decision that you are going to make."

Let that question sit with you for a bit. Journal anything that comes to mind: any area that you want to give to God but haven't, or any area that you need help saying, "Not my will but yours."

Rhonda had an eternal perspective. She knew this world was not her home. I am so comforted to know that even though we may lose those we love here on this earth, if they know Jesus as their Lord, then we will all be reunited again in a perfect place. Death on this earth is not the final end. We have so much more waiting on us in heaven. Soooo much good stuff. A place is waiting for us with no death and no disease!

Another bit of wisdom that Robyn gave me in our talk was a quote from her mom, "Don't let your mind go where God's grace isn't yet." God's grace will cover us and give us strength when we need it. But to allow our minds to keep going to the 'what if's' does no good. It robs us of the joy of today.

Write a prayer to God. He has the power to give us peace. He has the power to comfort us. Nothing is too big for God. He has overcome Death. Death is not the end. Allow your prayer to express your thankfulness as well as your burdens. God wants to hear it all. He loves you so much.

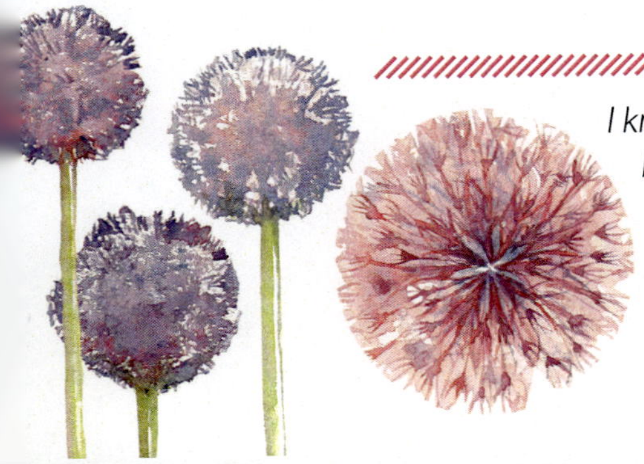

I know this can be a hard topic to talk about, however, talking can sometimes be healing. I encourage your small group to discuss your fears of the future. Then if you are comfortable, have a time of prayer over each person in your group. Matthew 18:20 says, "When two or more are gathered in my name, there I am with them." So gather up and pray. There is power in your prayers!

HANDWRITING Technique

Fill the Format

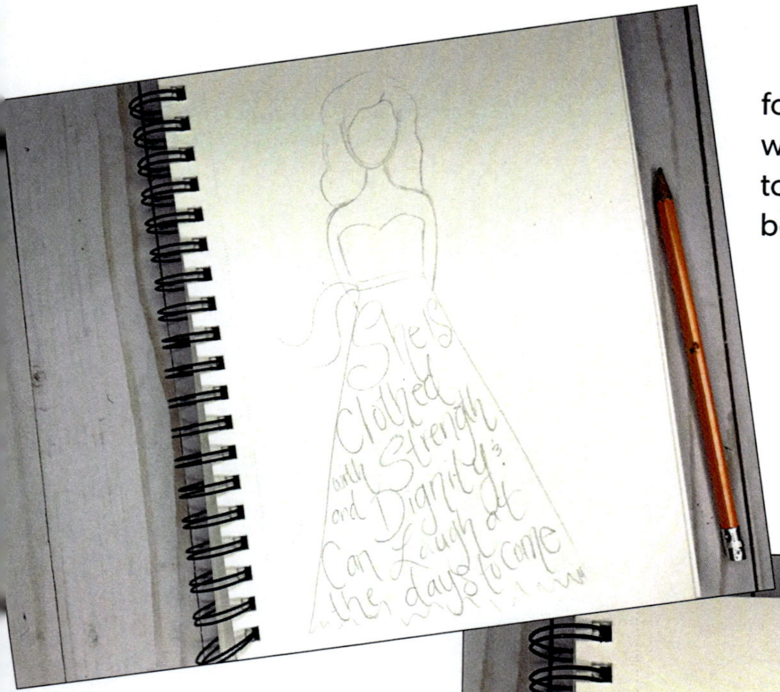

This week I want you to practice filling the format with your lettering. In this case, we will draw a picture of a girl and I want you to practice filling your letters from top to bottom, left to right!

1 Use pencil first.

2 Then go back in with your Sharpie to thicken some of your letters.

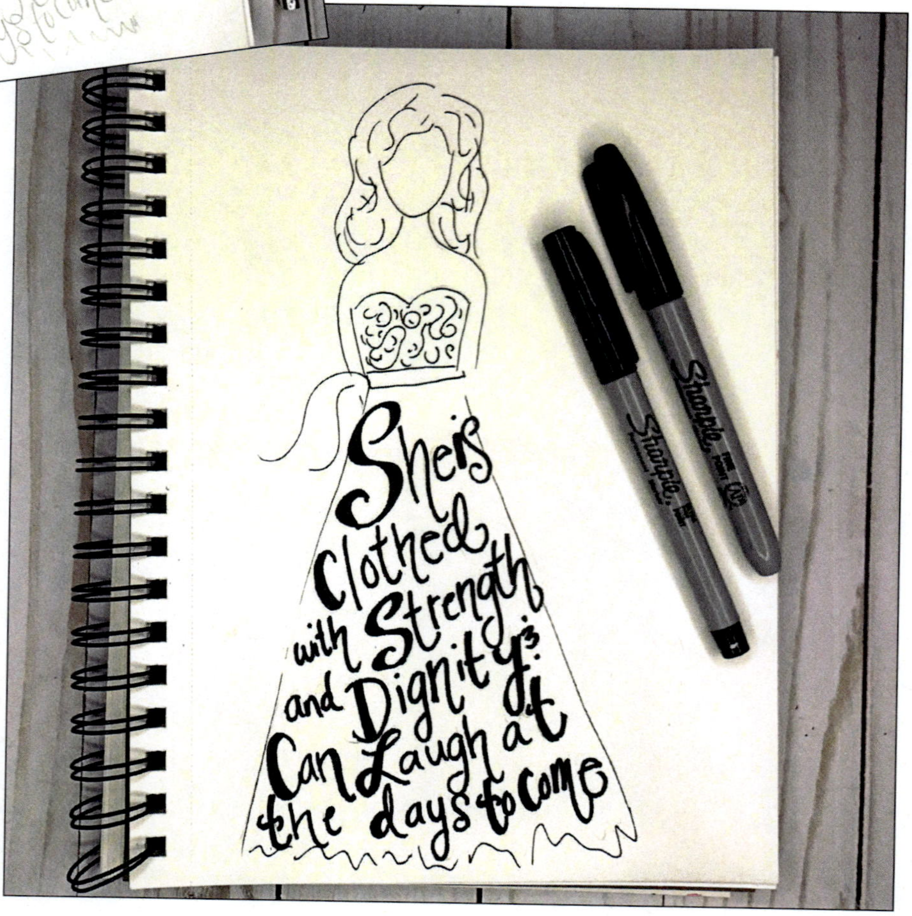

Practice here

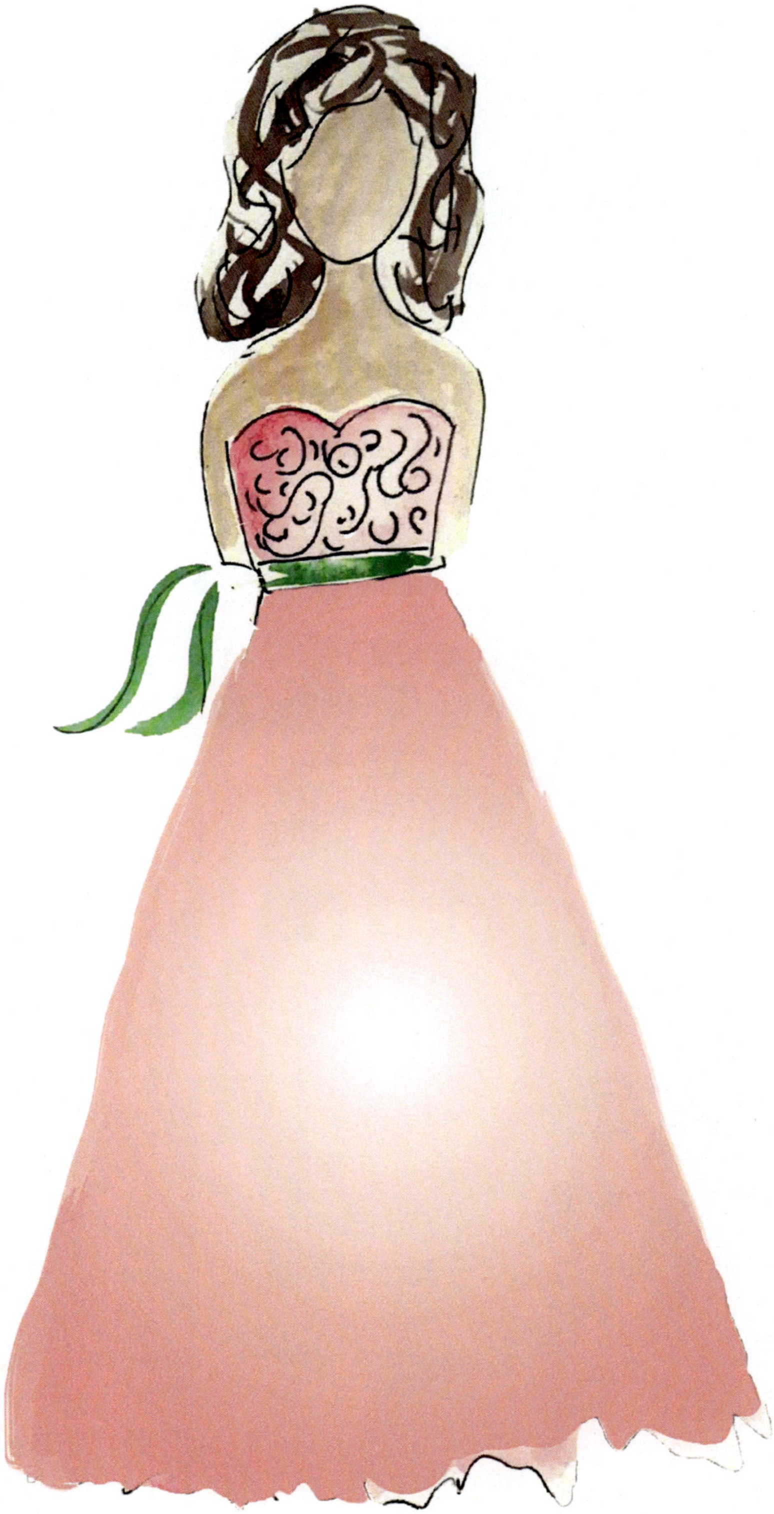

ART Technique Fading Watercolor

SUPPLIES: Sharpie • Watercolor • Watercolor Paper • Micron Pen

After you have drawn your girl and filled the format with your lettering, now it's time to paint!!

1 Add pink along the edges of the dress.

2 Then simply add plain water. Don't get any more pigment on your brush. You should see that the color begins to fade towards the middle of the dress. Adding water is an easy way to make watercolor fade to a lighter shade!!

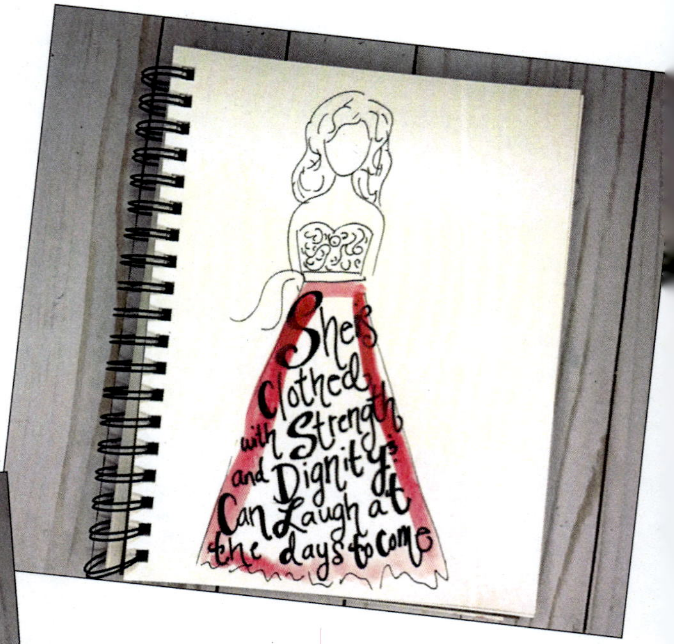

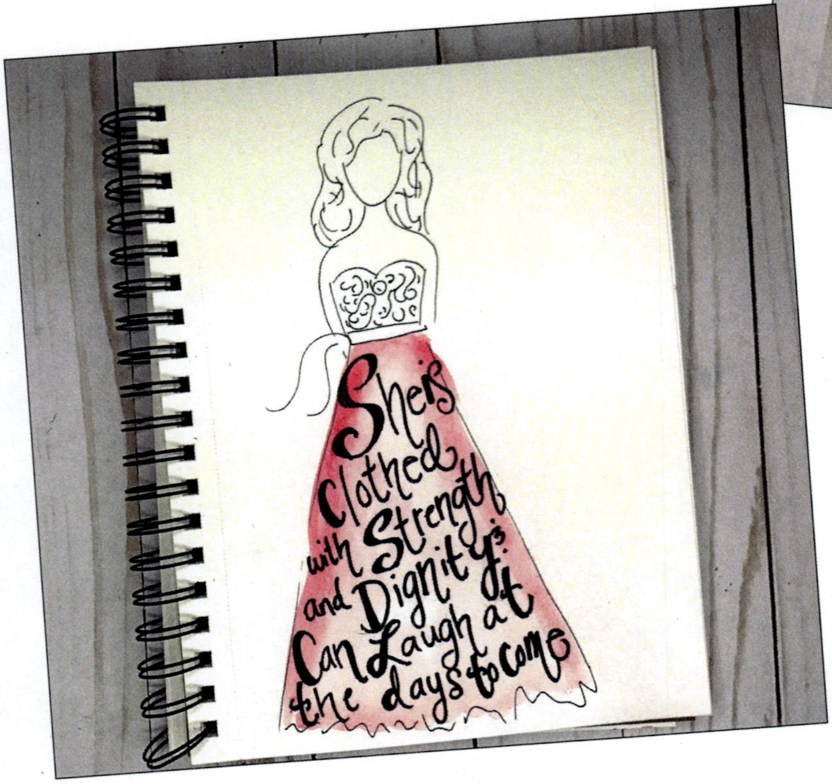

3 You can do this on the top of the dress too!

4 Then have fun adding color to the rest of your page!!

Proverbs 31:25

Ladies, my prayer for you is that you are truly allowing God to take your fears and anxieties so that you can become this lady right here. You can truly have no worries of the days to come because you know God's got it!!

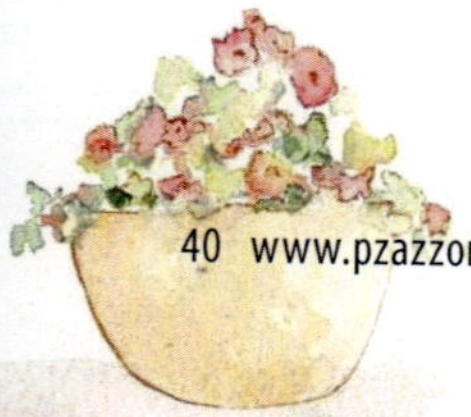

Your Finished Picture

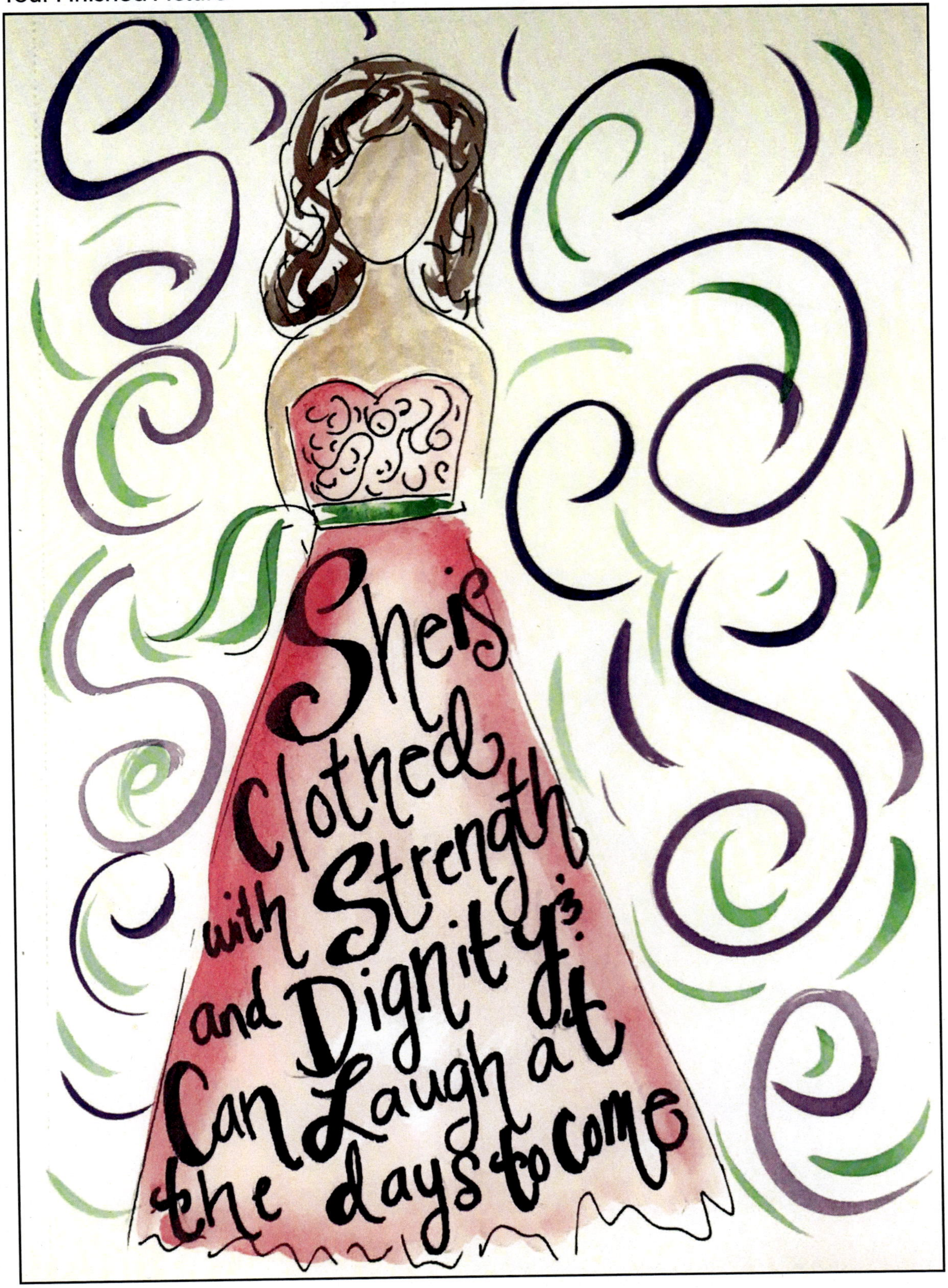

Extra Practice

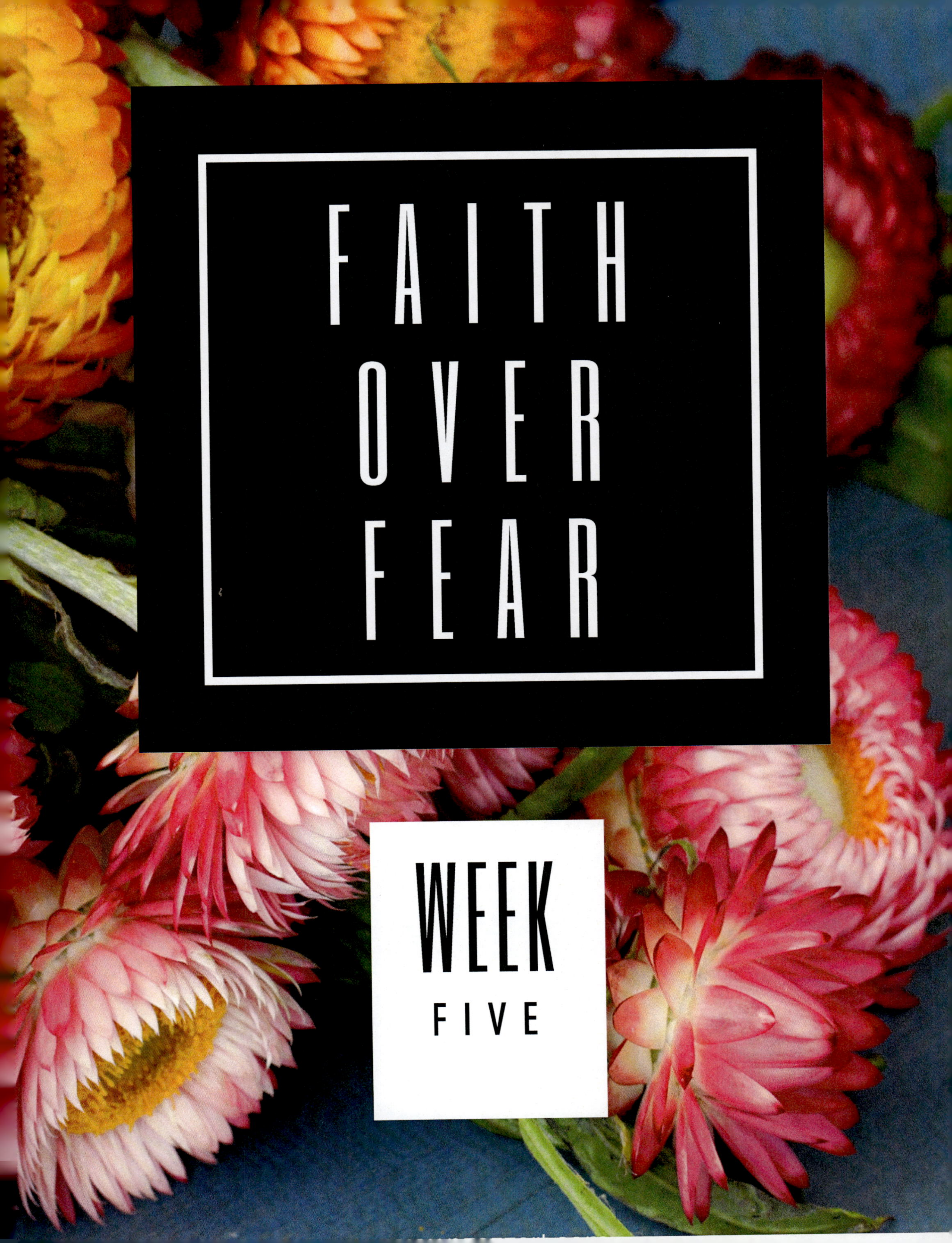

FAITH OVER FEAR

WEEK FIVE

WEEK FIVE: FEAR OF NOT HEARING GOD

Have you ever heard people say, "God has called me to ______" and thought to yourself, "Well, that's great for you, but I don't think God has *called* me to anything?"

I know I felt like that for a while. I didn't seem to have any notable Christian talents or burdens. (A burden is what makes your heart ache and you desperately want to see something done about it... i.e. poverty, hungry children, abused women, at-risk teenagers, teenagers in general, elderly, the "me" generation, etc.) God didn't *call* me to seminary like he did for so many of my friends. He didn't *call* me to move overseas and serve in the foreign mission field. He didn't *call* me to work in a church. He didn't give me a singing voice, so I sure knew He wasn't calling me to a worship team of any sort.

I knew I loved God, but for a long time I didn't feel there was anything special that He wanted me to do. Friend, I want you to know that if you feel like that too, you are not alone. But, I've got some good news! God does have a plan for you.

Jeremiah 29:11 says:

____

____

____

God has already equipped you with gifts and talents that he is going to use in mighty ways if you will follow his lead and step into what He's got for you!

First, let's look at what He has called **every** Christian to do. Put these verses in your own words. What does this mean for you?

Matthew 28:19

____

____

Acts 1:8

____

____

Mark 16:15

____

____

Romans 10:14-15

____

____

Every Christian is called to tell others about Jesus. How will unbelievers know if we don't tell them? But if you're anything like me, you really want to hear God's specific plan for YOU.

Read Genesis 1:28. God said to ______ over the fish in the sea and the birds in the sky and over every living creature that moves on the ground. This was one of the marching orders God gave Adam. From the very beginning, God told mankind to "rule over." From the very beginning, he expected his people to be leaders. Please don't take this as "ruling" over other people necessarily. God was telling them to rule over what he had given them: to be a leader and manage what was freely given, the land.

Very often, when we start listing these out, and simultaneously asking God to show us His specific assignment for us... we start to see how He has already begun working in us and pulling us toward the assignment or "call" that He has for us. And the cool thing is that this life is a journey. It's not a one-time assignment and that's your only goal for the rest of your life.

God continues to move you forward if you keep taking the next step in faith.

What has God given you? Maybe in your area of influence? Your talents? Your burdens? List them here.

My God-given talents: ____________________

The skills I've developed over the years : ____________________

My areas of influence: ____________________

My burdens: ____________________

Let me show you how this exercise helped me to see God's call in my life: to open P'zazz.

My God-given talents: paint, draw, being creative

The skills I've developed over the years: teaching, art, classroom management, creating lesson plans, encouraging kids to be the best they can (I was an Elementary Education major and taught school at the time. Do you see how God was preparing me?!)

My areas of influence: Kids. I love kids and kids love me.

My burden: Kids. I wanted kids to see that they have so much potential in them. I wanted them to be problem-solvers, but more than that I wanted them to 'wow' themselves. I wanted to encourage kids and build them up. I wanted them to be future leaders who had high morals and a love for giving instead of a love for getting. I wanted them to quit believing the lies that they aren't good enough and instead pour truth into them that they are loved, and valued, and talented!

And at the same time, I had a burden for my own child who was on the way. I wanted to build her up. To be there for her. To raise a little girl to the best of my ability.

When you read over my list it may make perfect sense on this side of things that I should open an art studio. It's a place to teach, to create, to build kids up, and to stay home with my little girl during the day. However, it wasn't clear to me at the time. I had to listen to God, the prompting of the Holy Spirit, and even others who began suggesting that I start teaching art.

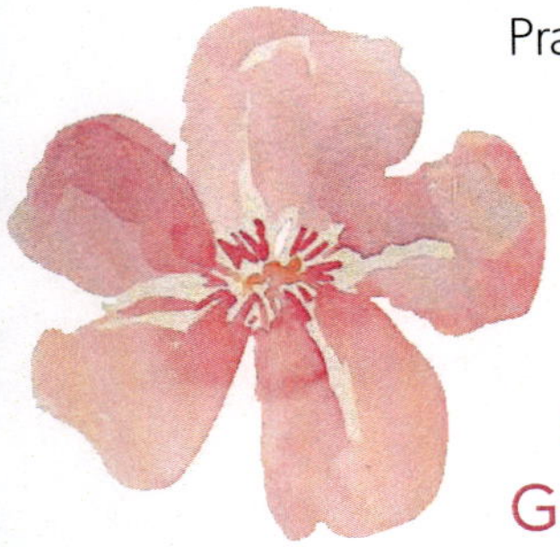

Prayer has got to be the main part of hearing God. We have to talk to Him and listen to Him.

Read John 10:27 and write it here: ____________________

____________________ We have to "LISTEN."

So how in the world can we hear God? The good news is that God still speaks!! He has a personal word for you. So how does God speak today?

____

____

To hear God, you have to come to Him with a cleansed heart.

You have to confess to him any places in your life where you have been disobedient. Often times, God won't tell me my next steps if He sees I haven't been faithful in the first steps. For example, there are tons of things written in the Bible that we don't have to guess about. A few things that we know God has told us to do are: forgiving others, tithing, not being jealous of what others have, honoring our parents, being truthful in all our dealings, not putting other "gods" in front of God. Are the 10 commandments ringing a bell? (Exodus 20:2-17 and Deuteronomy 5:6-21) If we have any of these sins in our life, then there is a block between us and God. Take some time now to confess to God any sin or disobedience in your life.

Once you approach God with a cleansed heart, these are the primary ways God still speaks today:

The Bible

The first and clearest way he speaks is through HIS WORD - The Bible! This is the baseline for everything else. The Holy Spirit will never lead you toward something that contradicts the Bible. If the advice you are getting from other people goes against what the Word of God says, then it isn't Godly advice. This is one reason it's so important to read God's Word. He has so much to say to us and teach us through the Bible!!!

Prayer

We have got to quiet ourselves with God. I like to keep a prayer journal to help keep my thoughts focused. I begin with listing what I am thankful for, then I confess what needs to be confessed, then I write my requests, and I leave some blank space to write down what I feel I hear God saying. Of course you don't have to keep a journal. But communication with God and having an actual relationship with Him is vital. In order to hear Him, you have to talk with Him. And that's all prayer is! Talking with God!

The Holy Spirit

John 14:26 "But the Advocate, the Holy Spirit, whom the Father will send in my name, will teach you all things and will remind you of everything I have said to you."

Acts 1:8 " You will receive power when the Holy Spirit comes on you..."

The Holy Spirit helps us understand the scriptures, helps remind us of what God has said, and prompts us (that little nudge in your heart).

He is our counselor (John 14:16) and our guide.

Remember though, the Holy Spirit will never guide you toward something that is against God's Word. Always check what you think the Holy Spirit is saying to you against the Bible.

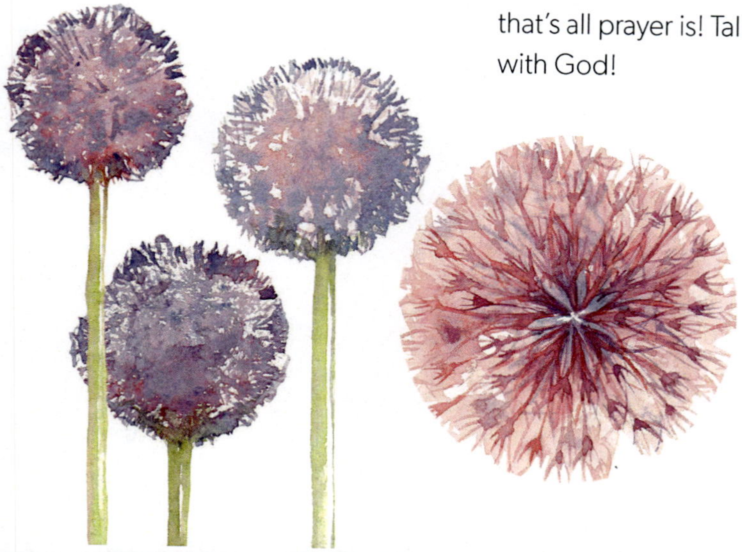

Other People

God still uses other people to speak! Countless pastors, speakers, friends, and books have helped me hear God more clearly. It's wise to listen to Godly counsel. But once again, always check it against God's Word. There are a lot of speakers, teachers, and even pastors today that are teaching things contradictory to what the Bible says. Don't just assume that people in a high position or who have lots of social media influence are right. Often times I have seen other people start with good intentions but end up teaching a very watered-down version of truth. Lots of influencers are saying what you want to hear, but beware… false truths lead to destruction.

Read 2 Timothy 4:3 and record it here "For the time will come when people will not put up with _________ doctrine. Instead, to suit their ______ desires, they will gather around them a great number of teachers to say what _____ itchy ears _________ ." God saw this one coming. It doesn't surprise Him. That's why He warned us about false speakers and teachers.

Yes, God still speaks through other people. But listen carefully and ask the Holy Spirit for wisdom to determine if what they say is truly from God.

Circumstances

God will orchestrate circumstances sometimes so that there is no denying that He is at work.

I would love to be in your small group and share stories of when I have clearly heard God. I would love to hear your stories too! Share some times when you have heard God clearly with your group.

What are you seeking to hear from God now? Share with your group. If your group feels comfortable, have a prayer time over each other. Also, assign prayer partners and commit to praying with them, and for them, this week.

God wants you to hear from Him.
Jeremiah 19:23 "You will seek and find me when you seek me with all your heart."

Handwriting Technique Thicken and Fil

In this picture we are going to thicken the letters like we've done before, but this time we will add in some color instead of filling it with our Sharpie!

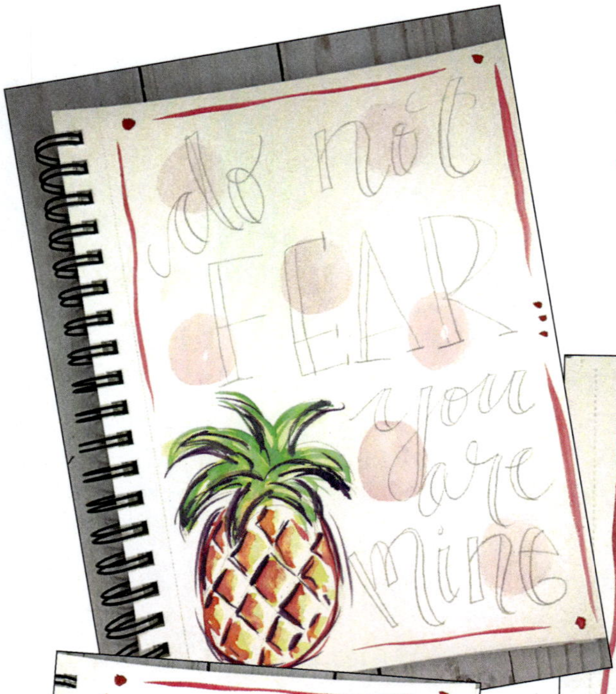

1 Pencil your lettering in first.

2 Go back and thicken your downstrokes with pencil.

3 Outline with Sharpie.

4 Fill with watercolor paint!

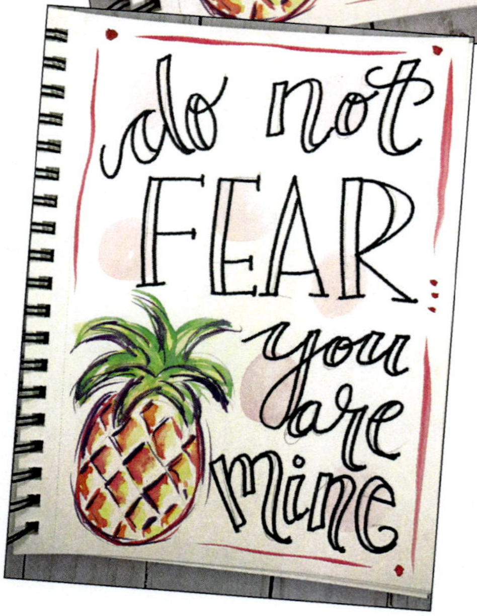

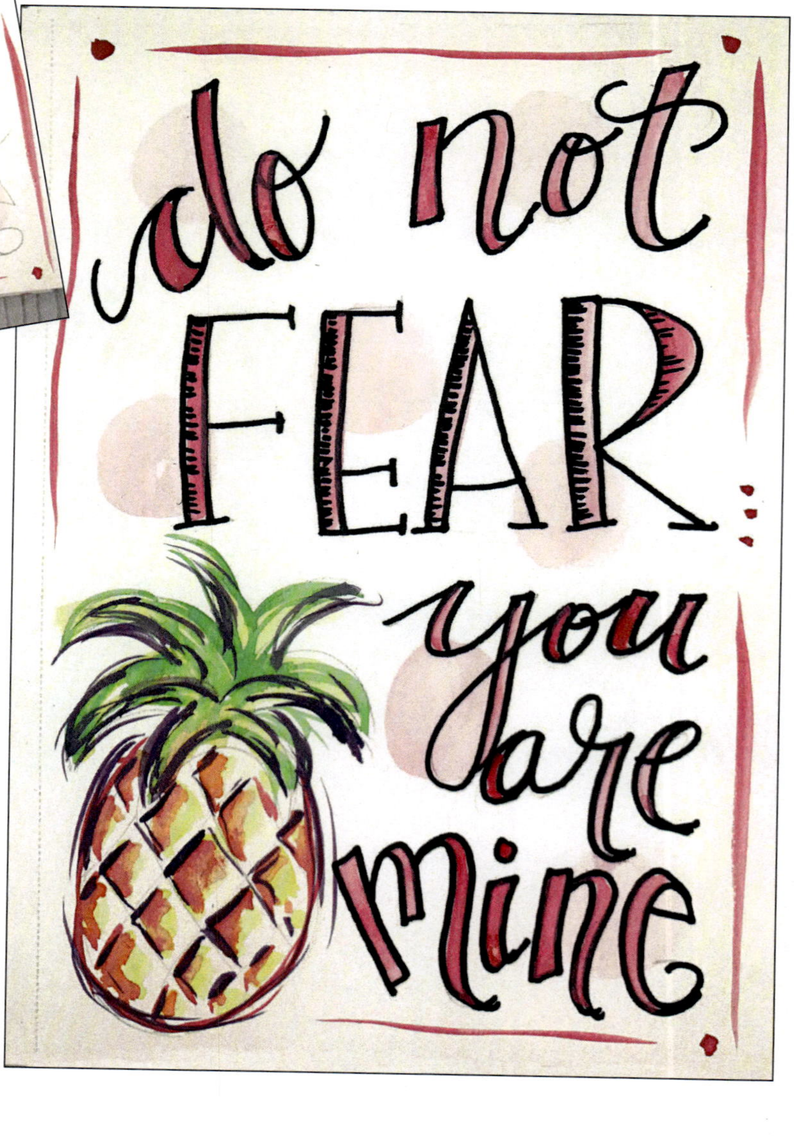

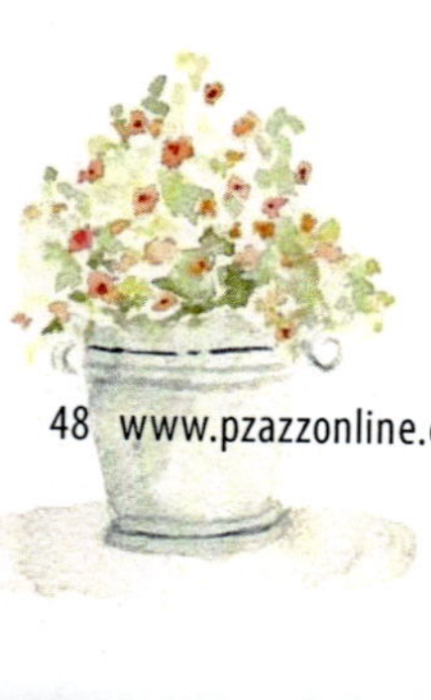

Practice here

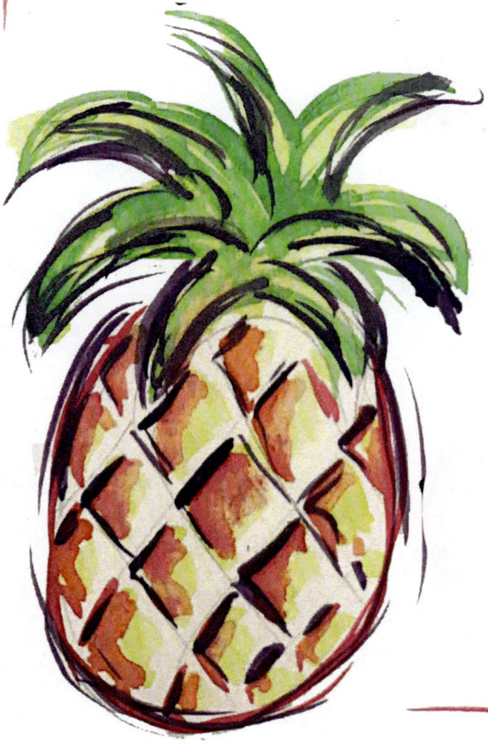

ART Technique Layering Color

SUPPLIES: Sharpie • Pencil • Watercolor • Small Watercolor Brush

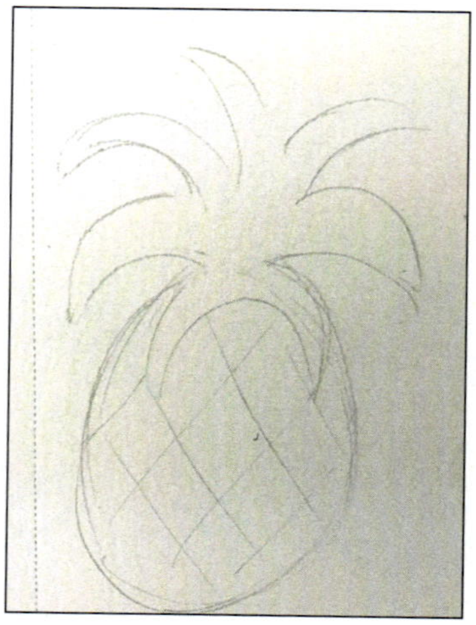

1 Sketch your pineapple with pencil first.

2 Add yellow into the diamond shapes on the pineapple. Leave some white between each diamond shape.

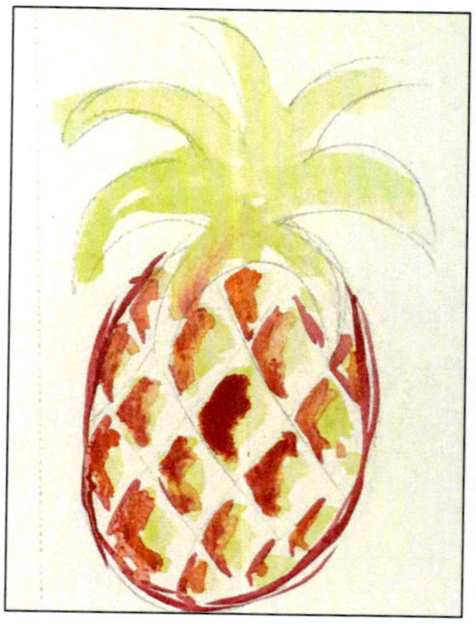

3 While it's still wet, add in orange and pink on the left side of the diamonds. Plus, you can use that pink to put a light little outline on the oval shape the pineapple.

4 Next, fill in the top of your pineapple with some yellow, followed by some green strokes.

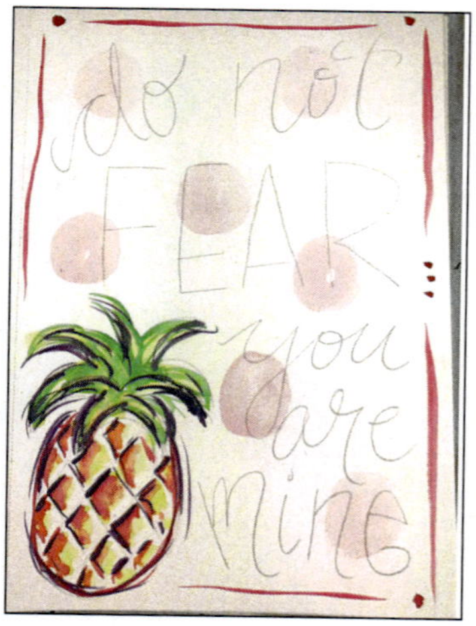

5 While I am waiting on the pineapple to dry, I add in my border and light pink dots in the background.

6 Once the pineapple is VERY dry, I can use a small brush and some purple to add some definition. Notice that the purple is going on the left side of the diamond shapes inside the pineapple. It's not a solid outline.

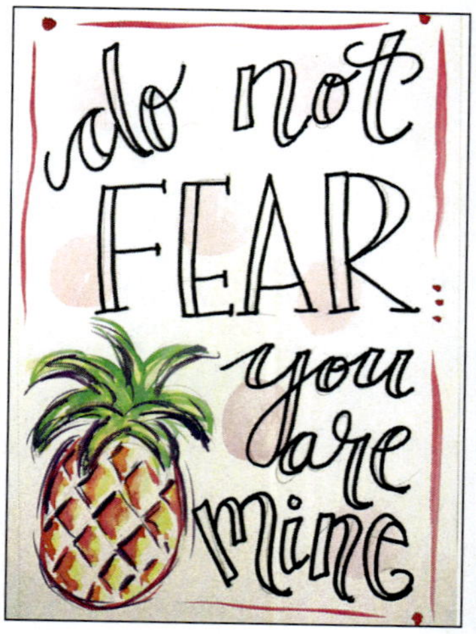

Isaiah 43:1

Notice that I am just putting a portion of the verse here on this art card. Be sure to watch the video to see how I like to write the whole verse out on a separate page in my watercolor sketchbook!!

Your Finished Picture

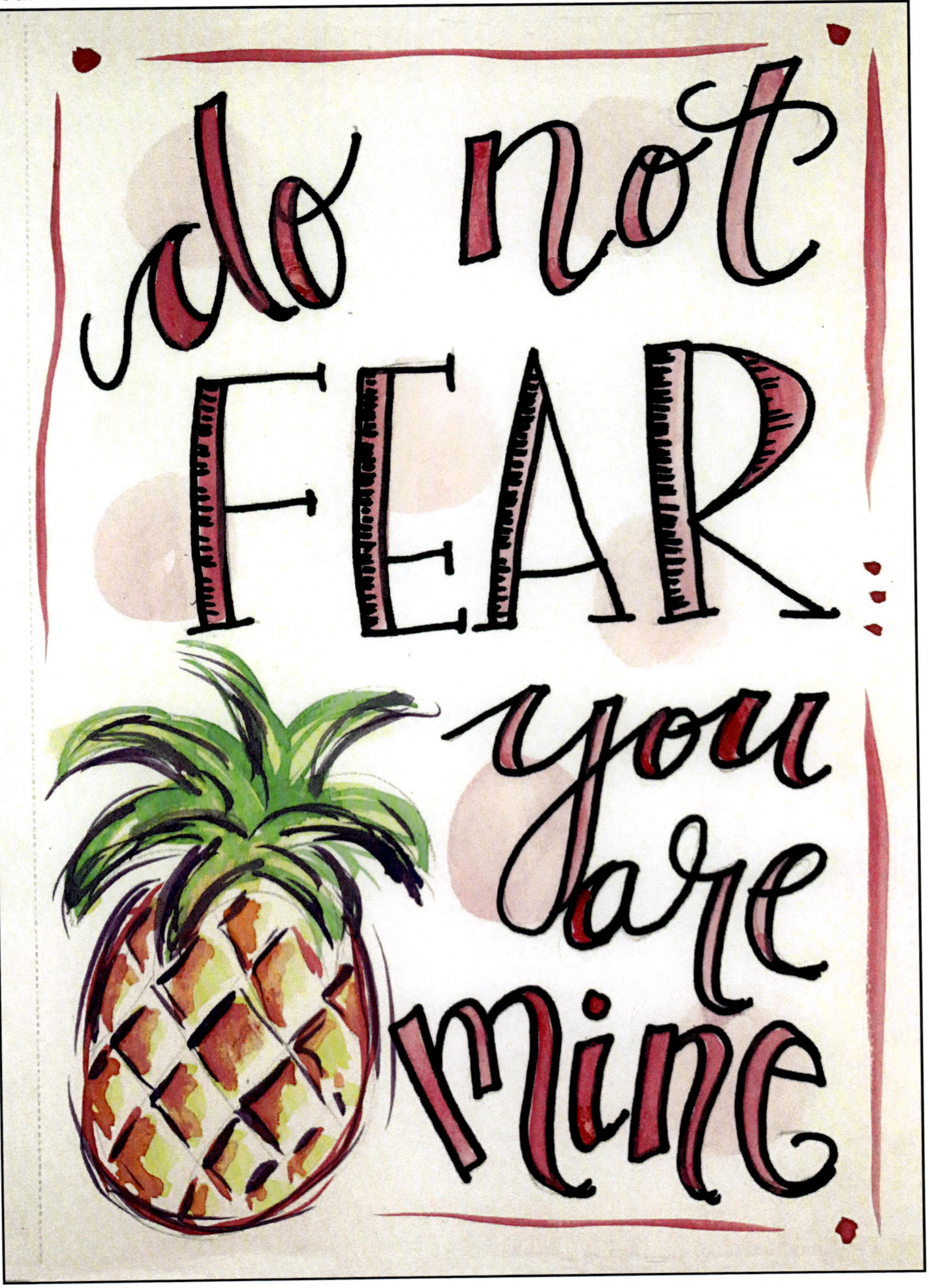

Extra Practice

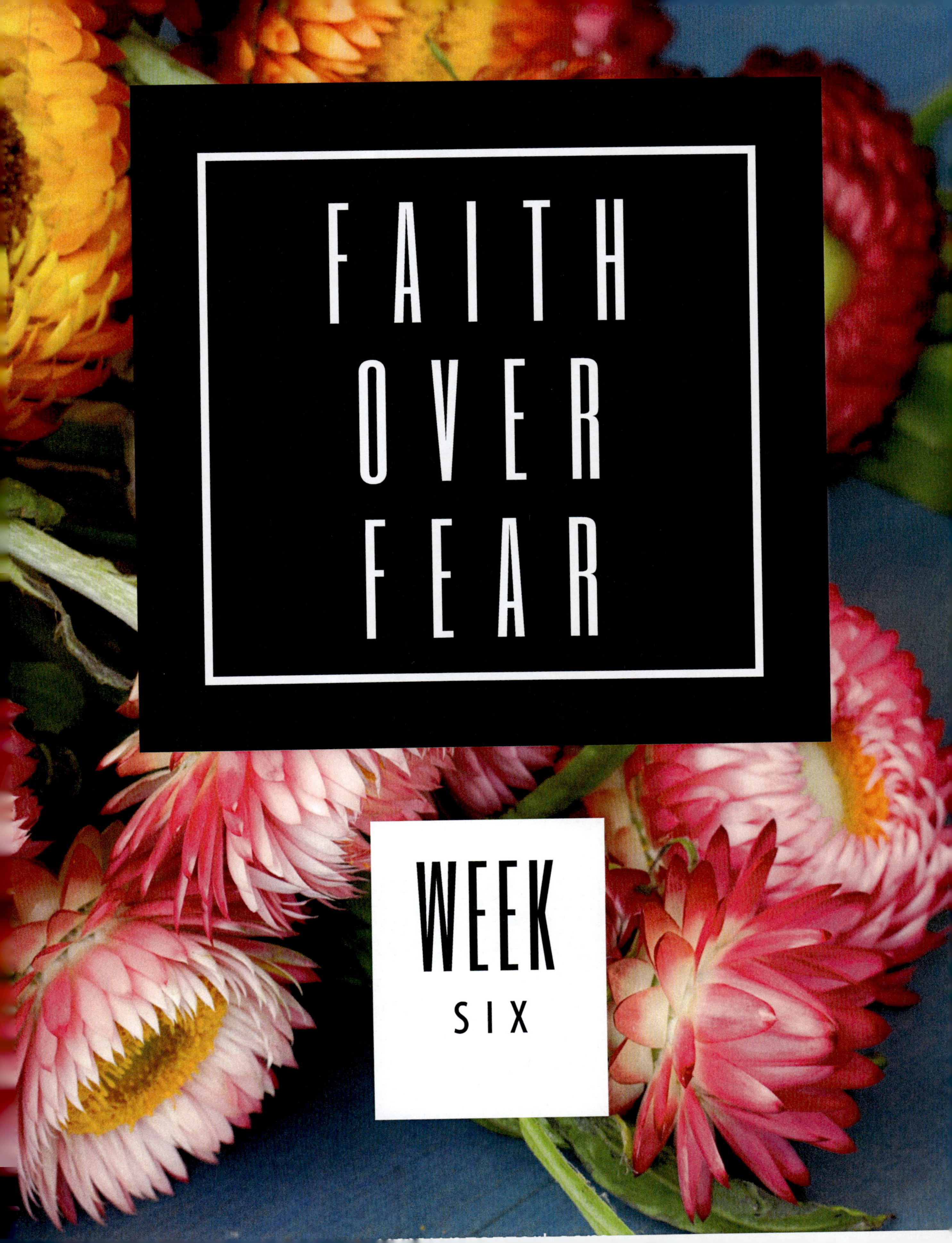

FAITH OVER FEAR

WEEK SIX

WEEK SIX: TOES IN THE WATER

I'm a little bit sad that this is our last lesson.

I feel like our time together has been fun and rich. If you've been working in groups, I hope that you have allowed yourself to get real and honest with your group. If you've done this on your own, I hope you got real and honest with yourself.

There are so many fears that we didn't even begin to touch on during this 6-week session. Some of my personal fears and anxieties are fear of heights, sometimes anxiety when driving, extreme anxiety when night driving, and gosh! ... the stories I could tell about driving at night in the pouring down rain... talk about paralyzed in fear!! ***Regardless of your personal struggle with fear or anxiety, I hope you have seen the benefit of memorizing God's word.***

We've made pretty little art cards filled with scripture or reminders of what God says. This hasn't been just for fun. These art cards are to be put all over your house, on your mirror, in your car, wherever you need them. Get some washi tape and tape them to the walls. We want these truths in our minds so that when we need them we can recall them and recite them.

Y'all, even this weekend as I was driving down the road by myself at night I had to literally, out loud, again... recite, *"I will trust in the Lord and not be afraid, the LORD HIMSELF is my strength and defense..." Isaiah 12:2.* It doesn't make sense why fear comes over me sometimes, why my palms start sweating, and why I want to slow down to 20 miles an hour.

I have no idea why this happens sometimes and why other times I'm just fine. But what I do know is that when I start speaking scripture, out loud, over my situation and BELIEVING scripture... then slowly and very surely, the fear starts to dissipate.

When I BELIEVE that God has gone before me and prepared the road ahead of me, and that He really is defending me and giving me strength, then that belief and that reality gives me strength.

But what happens when we still feel the fear even though we know what God says? Let's look to scripture for that. Read Joshua 3 (the whole thing).

Summarize what you just read. If there was anything in particular you noticed or that stood out, record that here too.

____

____

____

____

____

Now focus on Joshua 3:15. When did the water from upstream stop flowing?

____

____

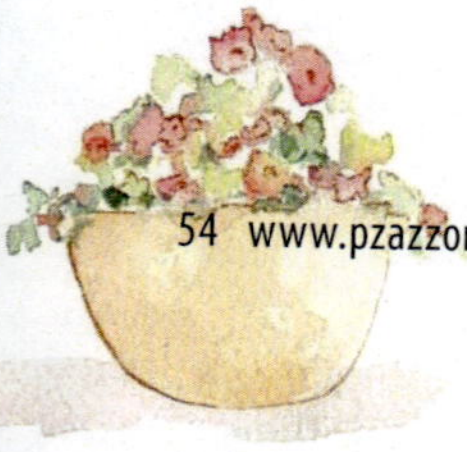

Put yourself in the priest's shoes for just a bit.

You pick your right foot up to take a step... nothing special is happening.

Your right foot is swinging forward... nothing is happening.

Oh gosh, you are about to put your foot down right on the water's edge and it doesn't look like anything is happening. Do you pause and hold your foot in the air until God moves, or do you do what you've been told, even though it looks like there is still water there? The priest's feet touched the water's edge. They stepped in BEFORE the water stopped. BEFORE there were obvious signs that God was about to move. BEFORE they knew it was gonna be safe. BEFORE they saw the whole picture, they took the first step. They put their toes in the water. Then God showed up!!! Over and over again, we come back to the fact that

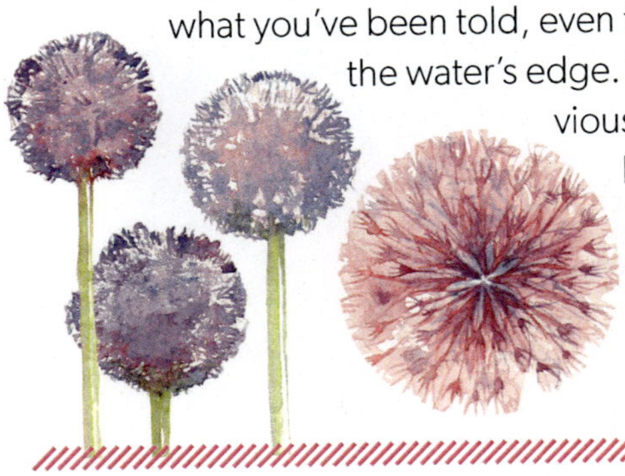

" ______________ ___________ it is IMPOSSIBLE to please God"
(Hebrews 11:6)

And what is Faith? Hebrews 11:1: "Now faith is the confidence in what we hope for and assurance about what we ______ _______ _______ !!! Faith is the key that activates so much in our life. We have to believe God, even when we don't see the whole path. We have to take the step of faith even when we feel fear. Sometimes we have to just do it when we're scared.

Feeling Fear about finances?

In FAITH, do money God's way and watch how God provides. Watch how Malachi 3:10 plays out.

Feeling Fear about taking the next step towards what you are called to do?

Do it anyway. **In FAITH**, take the next step even though you can't see two steps ahead. Believe Jeremiah 29:11 that God has plans for you, to prosper you, and not to harm you.

Feeling FEAR about the future and the unknown?

In FAITH, trust Romans 8:28 that all things work together for good for those that love God.

Feeling Fear of what others think?

In FAITH, believe Psalm 139:14 that you are fearfully and wonderfully made and all of God's works are wonderful, including YOU!!

It's a choice to choose Faith Over Fear. It's a choice. It's not a feeling that is going to happen automatically. It's a choice. Know what God's Word says and choose to believe it! Y'all, there is power in belief!! And if you have any specific prayer needs in the area of fear, I would love to pray for you. You can email me at kaseyau@gmail.com.

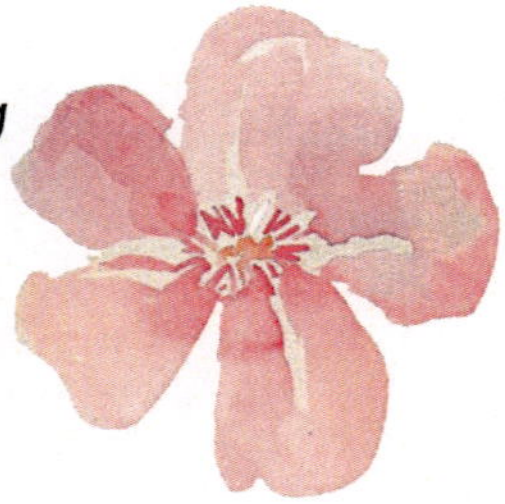

Handwriting Technique All Caps, Sloppy and Serifs

For this technique, just write big and quick. Let some words be in all caps and others in lower case.

Thicken your downstrokes and then add serifs to a few of the smaller letters!

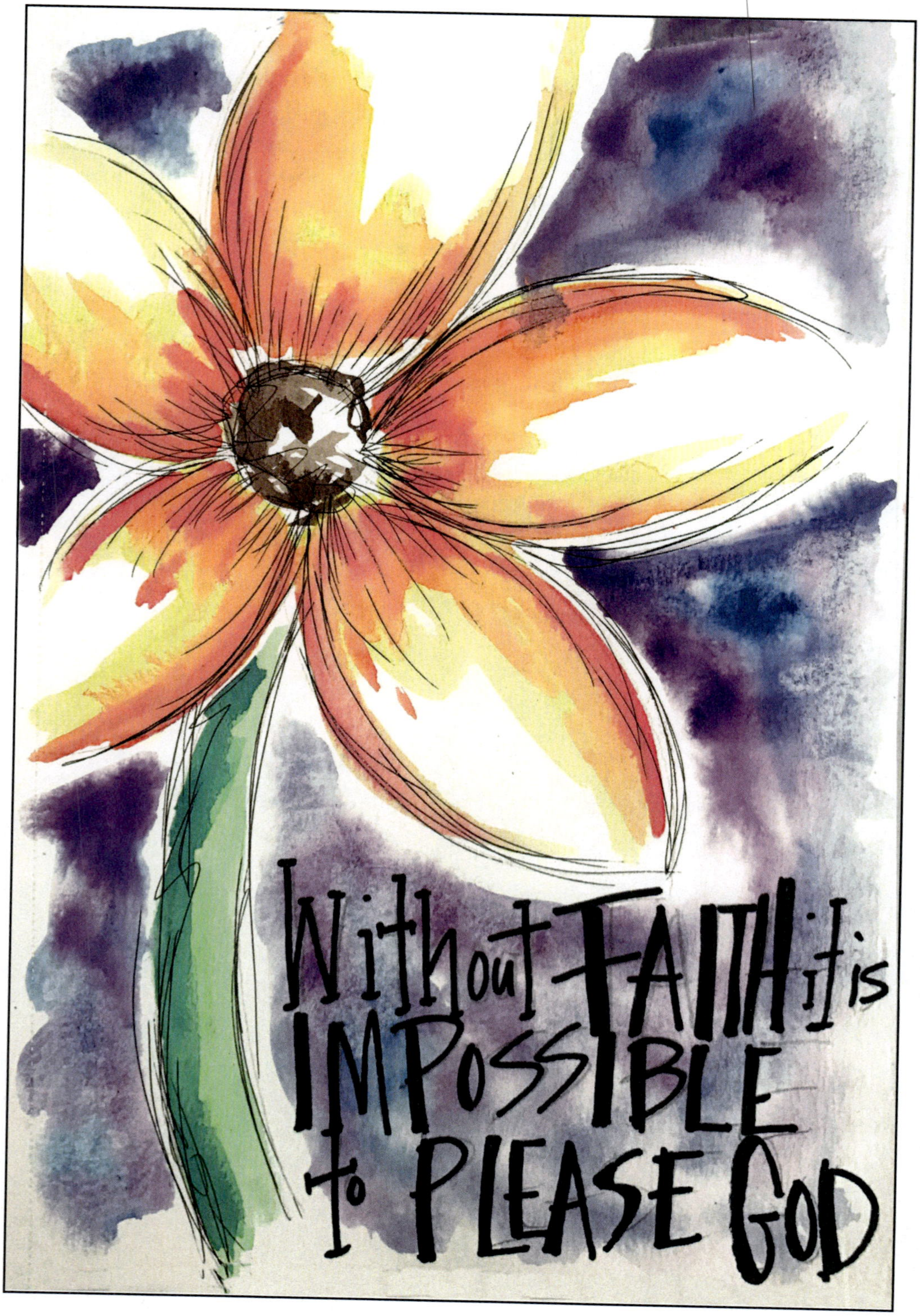

Practice here

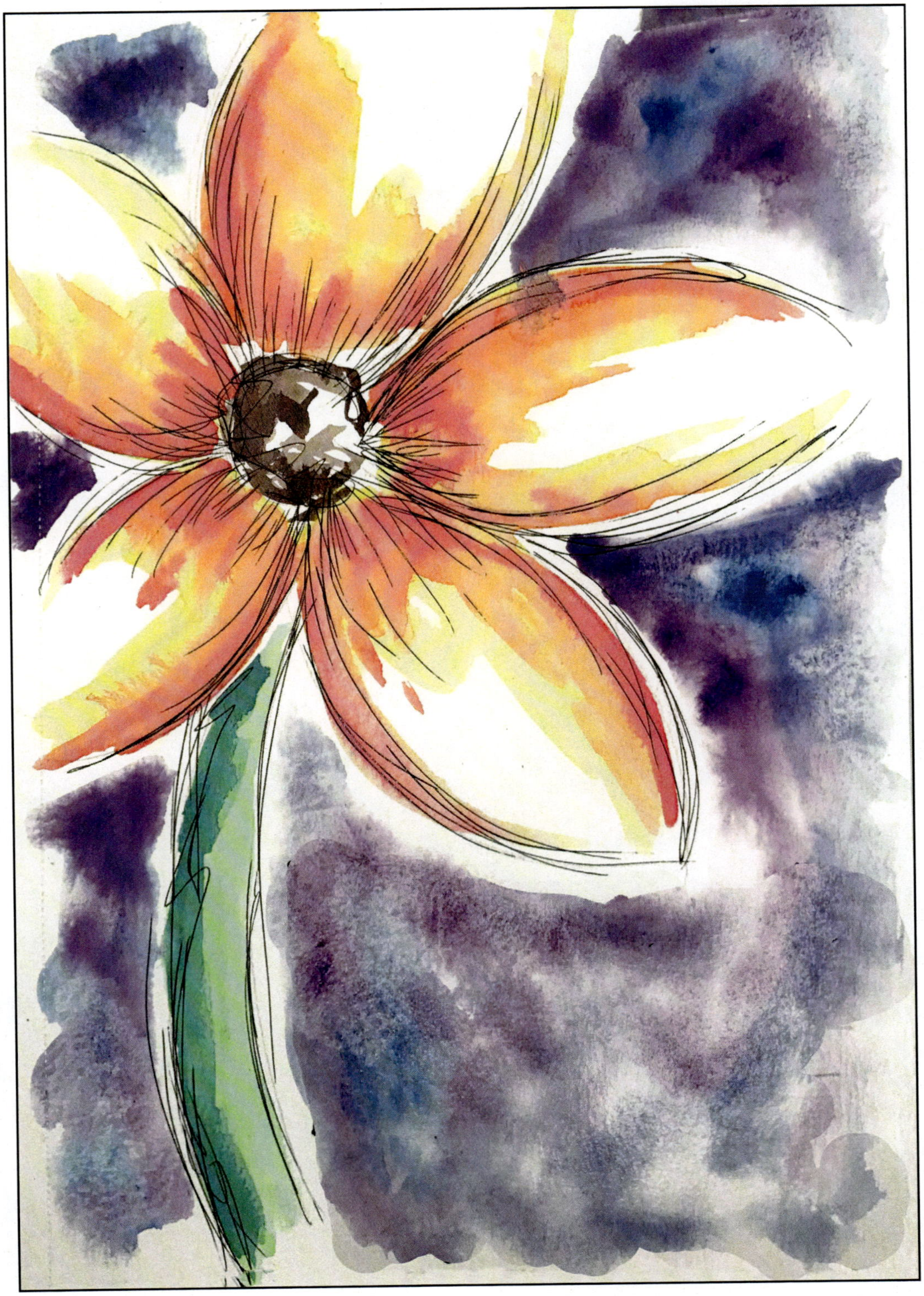

ART Technique Warm and Cool Colors, Wet-on-Wet, Adding Pen and Splatter

SUPPLIES: Watercolor • Watercolor Paper • Brush • Sharpie • Micron Pen

1 Lightly draw out your flower with pencil first.

2 Then add some yellow watercolor primarily one one side of the petals.

3 While the yellow is still wet you can add in some orange and pink.

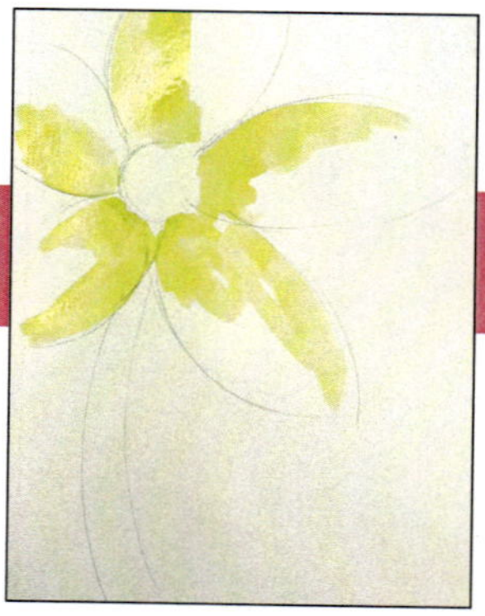

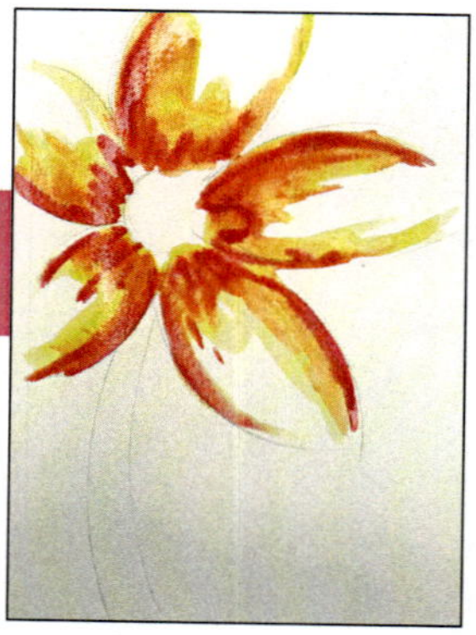

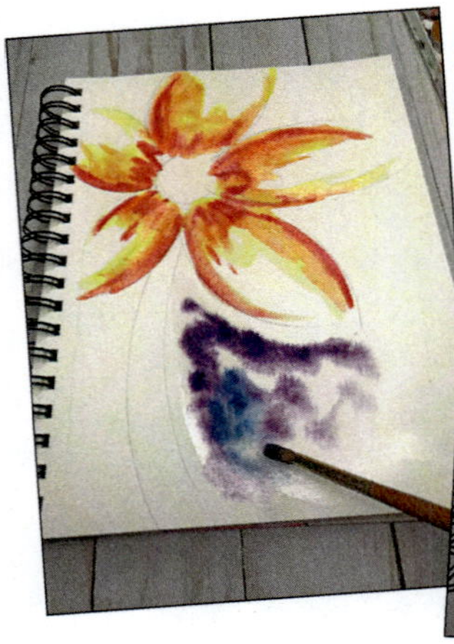

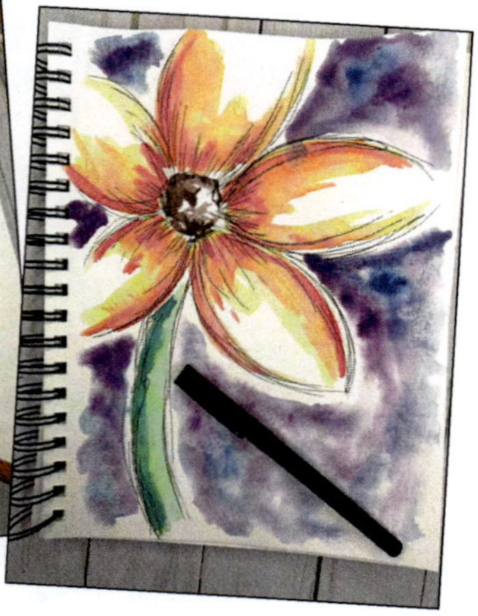

4 Next you will start on your background. We will be using the wet-on-wet technique again. Wet a small section of your background first. Then drop in blues and purples. (Notice how the colors really pop when you use warm colors on the flower and cool colors in the background!!)

5 Once the background is done, you can fill in green on the stem and scribbly brown in the center.

6 When it's COMPLETELY DRY, use a small pen to add in some outline and details.

7 Then you can add in your lettering.

8 After you are finished with everything else, get your brush really loaded with water and pigment and begin splattering!! *TIP: When splattering I always do my first splatter somewhere else besides my page. An extra sheet or a paper plate is best for practice. Also, the first splat is usually the biggest and sometimes it's best that the biggest splat isn't done on your page but on a practice page instead!*

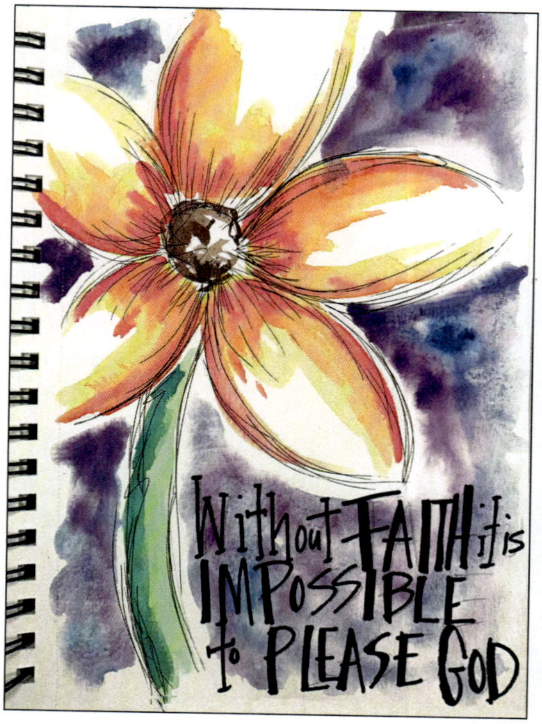

Your Finished Picture

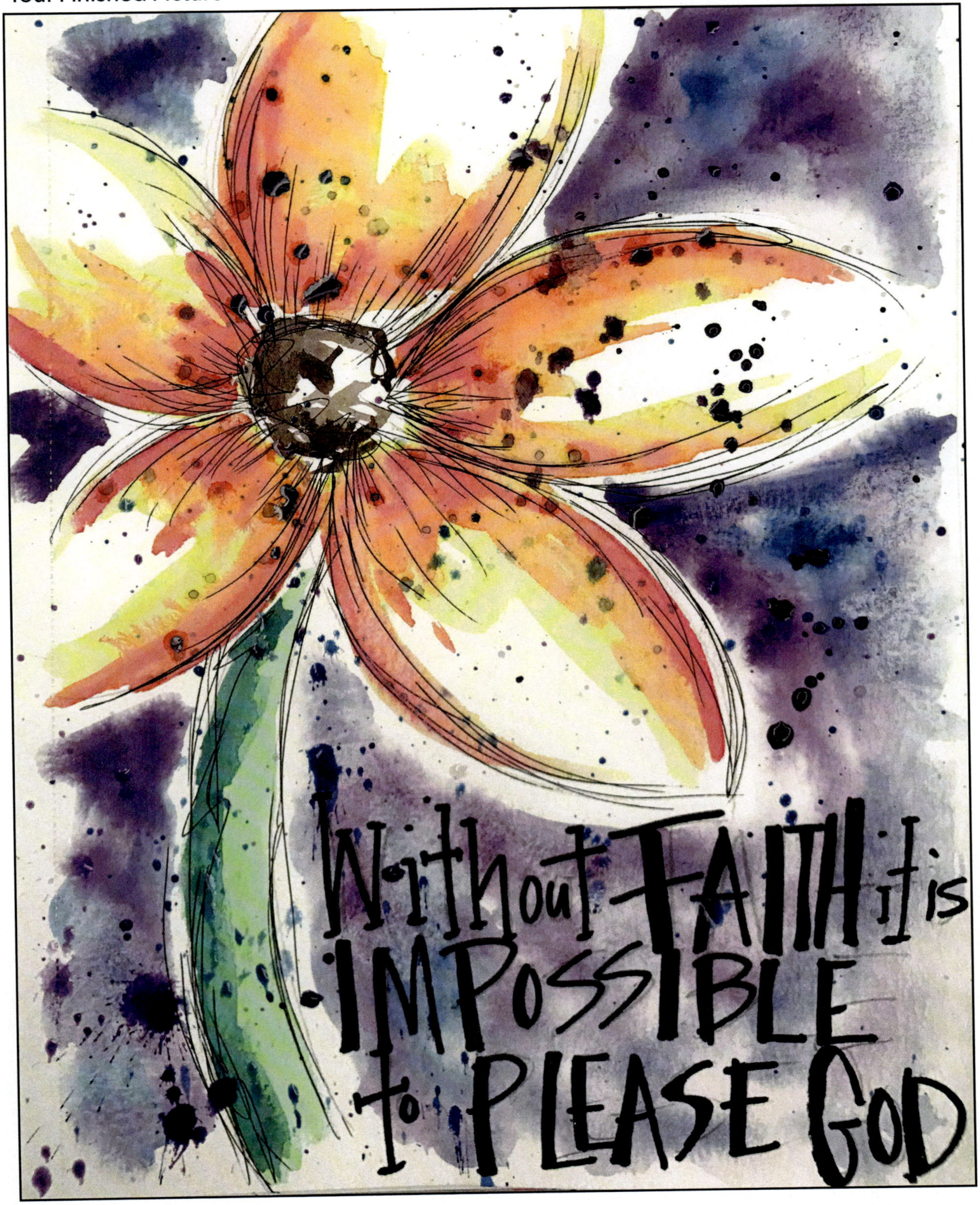

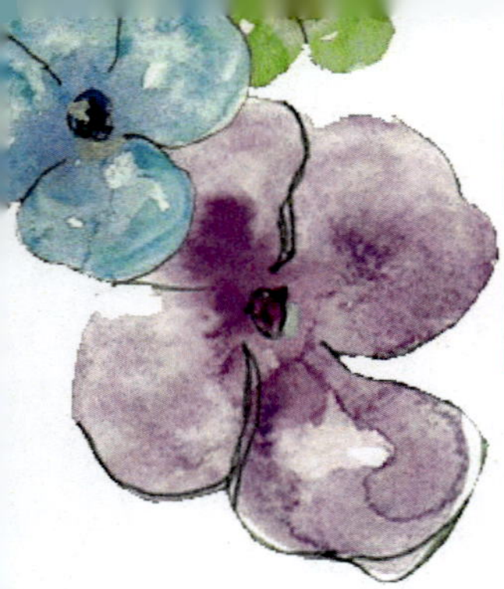

BELIEFS BASED ON SCRIPTURE

It's so important to know what scripture says about what we believe. Here are some key verses to help you understand what the Bible has to say on each topic. Feel free to use the blank space to look up verses and jot down what they say. Do your own research and dig in!

GOD

He has always existed in 3 persons - the Father, The Son, and the Holy Spirit. These three are co-equal and they are all One God.

Genesis 1:1

Genesis 1:26-27

Genesis 3:22

Psalm 90:2

Matthew 28:19

1 Peter 1:2

2 Corinthians 13:14

MAN

We are the supreme object of God's creation. Although humans have tremendous potential for good, we are impaired by an attitude of disobedience called "sin." This attitude separates man from God.

Genesis 1:27

Psalm 8:3-6

Isaiah 53:6A

Romans 3:23

Isaiah 59:1-2

ETERNITY

We will all exist either eternally in hell, separated from God by sin, or eternally in heaven with God through forgiveness and salvation in Christ. Heaven and Hell are real places of eternal existence.

John 3:16

1 John 2:25

1 John 5:11-13

Romans 6:23

Revelation 20:15

Matthew 25:31-46

JESUS

He is co-equal with God. He lived a sinless life in human flesh and offered himself as the perfect sacrifice for the sins of ALL people by dying on the cross. He arose from death after three days to show his power over sin and death. He ascended to Heaven and will return to earth again to reign as King of Kings and Lord of Lords.

Matthew 1:22-23

Isaiah 9:6

John 1:1-5; 14:10-30

1 Corinthians 15:3-4

Romans 1:3-4

Acts 1:9-11

Hebrews 4:14-15

1 Timothy 6:14-15

SALVATION

Man can never make up for his sin by self-improvement or good works. We can't "work" our way into heaven. Only by trusting in Jesus Christ as God's offer of forgiveness can we be saved from sin's penalty.

Romans 6:23

Ephesians 2:8-9

John 14:6

John 1:12

Titus 3:5

Romans 5:1

Galatians 3:26

THE BIBLE

It was written by human authors, under the supernatural guidance of the Holy Spirit. It is the supreme source of truth for Christian beliefs and living. Because it was inspired by God, it is truth without any mixture of error.

2 Timothy 3:16

2 Peter 1:20-21

2 Timothy 1:13

Psalm 119:105

Psalm 119:160

Psalm 12:6

Proverbs 30:5

THE HOLY SPIRIT

He is present in the world to make men aware of their need for Jesus Christ. He also lives in every Christian from the moment of salvation. He provides the Christian with power for living, understanding of spiritual truth, and guidance in doing what is right. The Christian seeks to live under the Spirit's control daily.

2 Corinthians 3:17

John 16:7-13

John 14:16-17

Ephesians 1:13

Galatians 5:25

Ephesians 5:1

Acts 1:8

1 Corinthians 2:12

1 Corinthians 3:16

ETERNAL SECURITY

Because God gives us eternal life through Jesus Christ, believers are secure in their salvation for eternity. Salvation is maintained by the grace and power of God, not by the efforts of the Christian.

John 10:29

2 Timothy 1:12

Hebrews 7:25

Hebrews 10:10, 14

1 Peter 1:3-5

If you are not yet a Christian and wondering how to become one, it's really pretty simple. It's simple, but not easy.

When you understand that you are indeed a sinner and in need of a Savior because there's no way you're getting to heaven on your own... simply cry out to Jesus. He is The Savior!!

When you confess with your mouth that Jesus is LORD and believe in your heart that God raised him from the dead, you will be saved! (Romans 10:9).

Just have a conversation with God through prayer. Ask for forgiveness of your sins. Tell him you do believe in Him and His power. Tell God you want to make him Lord of your life and you are ready to follow where He leads!!

Then, find a church that you can get plugged into to help you grow and learn more about God and His character!

85511900R00035

Made in the USA
San Bernardino, CA
20 August 2018